BLOCKCHAIN DESIGN SPRINT

An Agile Innovation Workbook

To Implement an Agile Design Sprint

For Your Blockchain Business

BY MOSES MA

FUTURELAB

For information contact :
breakthrough@futurelabconsulting.com
http://www.futurelabconsulting.com

ISBN-13: 978-1548592714
ISBN-10: 1548592714

First Edition: July 4, 2017

PRAISE

"Moses is off the charts, A-Triple Plus. I was blown away by his ability to lead, create, examine, challenge and push us for dynamic and innovative results."—*Lori Crever, SVP, Wells Fargo Bank*

"Moses is engaging, visionary, and truly inspiring. He helps people to see the possibilities that are out there in our interconnected world."—*Mark Resch, CEO CommerceNet*

"Attendees of Moses' workshop as part of our acclaimed HyperInnovation program have raved about the experience as 'Exhilarating!' 'Mindblowing!' and 'Bullseye!' He delivers breathtaking, thought provoking experiential learning."—*Sandra Bradley, Exec. Director, Center for Innovation, University of Wisconsin Business School*

Agile Innovation offers a new approach to innovation – by blending the key aspects of the Agile development process with the tenets of classical innovation methodology. The bottom line is that this is a very important book, and makes a strong case for a paradigm shift in the methodology of innovation, based on the Agile approach. This must read book is successful in practicing what it preaches – in not just preaching innovation but by demonstrating innovativeness – and deserves to be read carefully and digested thoroughly. - *Jeff Sutherland, Co-inventor of Scrum and CEO, Scrum Inc*

Agile Innovation promises to profoundly transform businesses and institutions. This must-read book is a strategic imperative for anybody aiming to successfully deliver new products or services in a brutally competitive, digitally-accelerated business world." – *Errol Arkilic, Co-creator of Innovation Corps at the National Science Foundation*

"This thought-provoking and inspirational book is a must read for anyone seeking to master the art and science of innovation and accelerated business development. Simply put, it's a map that will lead you and your organization to exponential breakthrough success in the new Digital Gold Rush." – *Jack Canfield, Best selling author of The Success Principles and Chicken Soup for the Soul*

*This book is dedicated to my amazing, inspiring
and transformational muse, Claire.*

PREFACE

OVER THE NEXT DECADE OR SO, we can look forward to another one-hundred-fold drop in the cost-to-performance ratio of computing and communications technology. This means that computers will become at least one hundred times more powerful, and communicating will become a hundred times less expensive than it is now. The result will be yet another cycle of disruptive change, and so we can look forward to someday seeing, with our very own eyes, city streets filled with driverless cars and trucks, universal smartphone usage (as of 2017, global smartphone market penetration finally hit 50%) with smartphones providing services that today we can hardly imagine, and much more.

Sometimes it's hard to believe that it's only been 25 years since Tim Berners-Lee made the World Wide Web available to the public. Yet it's difficult at a personal level to perceive the real rate of change, because our capacity to adapt increases organically. We live within a local frame of reference, but the aggregate impact of change is exponential, and it's affecting businesses, governments and people in fundamental ways. Products and services that were revolutionary two years ago are rendered obsolete if they don't adapt to market changes fast enough, attitudes and expectations change, new technologies emerge, and the overall vector of change continues to accelerate.

And as a result, humanity today creates as much information in two days now as we did from the dawn of civilization through 2003; tomorrow we'll do the same in a day, and eventually we'll do it in a matter of hours, and then minutes. Yes, for a large portion of the human population it really is an amazing time to be alive, but on the other hand, not everyone is enjoying this technology boom. We must anticipate even greater levels of turbulence, chaos, and market disruption than we've seen in the last decade.

And now, at the very leading edge of this tsunami of disruption is the blockchain.

This is a new digital gold rush, and it has started to yield ingenious and thought-provoking tools and applications that herald a new and mysterious decentralized world of information and commerce that is coming some day soon. If the full scope of the vision of blockchain technologies actually does come into existence, then the consequences will be massive and profound, and for any organization to succeed in this brave new blockchain-powered world, it will require an entirely new approach to adaptation, and thus to innovation. It is for this purpose that we've developed the Agile Innovation design sprint.

What is Agile innovation? It's a framework and a set of tools and techniques that combine a rigorous approach to innovation management in an adaptive framework, thus enabling you to make rapid innovation progress in a dynamic and fast-changing competitive landscape. All of which has, of course, become increasingly important in these challenging times of such great turbulence and uncertainty.

What is a design sprint? A design sprint is a six-step process framework that helps address critical business questions through proven approaches including ethnography, design thinking, rapid prototyping, user testing, enhanced storytelling technique, and innovation process evolution. The goal is to assist innovation teams to gain key realizations and reaching clearly defined goals and deliverables effectively and efficiently.

Our book *Agile Innovation*, published by Wiley and Sons in 2014, provides a detailed explanation and a guide for implementation of Agile innovation, while this workbook provides the hands-on tools you need to facilitate adoption throughout your organization. In this version of the workbook, we use the blockchain revolution as the focal point for understanding how the Agile Innovation sprint works.

The digital revolution is a tsunami of change that will likely be unstoppable, so your organization must similarly become unstoppable in its commitment, perseverance and creativity. You must let go of the comfort of linear thinking, idea killing, non-dynamic business processes, and even competitor-copying in the name of "best practices." Indeed, the very concept of "best practices" is not only deficient in a rapidly changing market, but is probably a recipe for slow failure. To succeed you must instead evolve to continuously improve and reinvent every practice, every product, and every service.

The thing we can reliably predict accurately is that change is accelerating. More waves of disruption are hurtling at us—robotics, artificial intelligence, quantum computing, genomic medicine, virtual and augmented reality, and some we don't yet have names for. It isn't going to stop, but the skills and tools that this workbook provides can be applied to all of these waves, at whatever the future throws at us. Agile innovation can become your surfboard, as it not only helps you to survive change, but to thrive in it. Mahalo!

CONTENTS

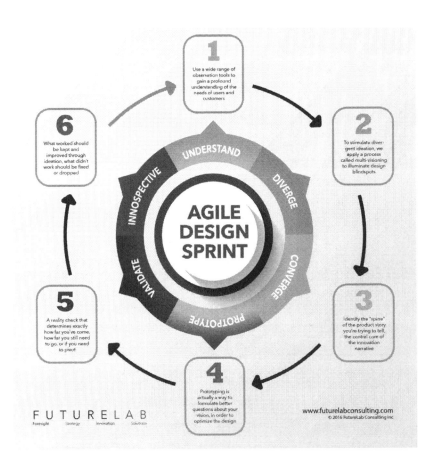

INTRODUCTION

I T IS INDISPUTABLE THAT THE GLOBAL convergence of computing miniaturization, personal computing technology, and Internet and wireless data services is inspiring a new digital age. However, the full impact of the Information Revolution is only beginning to be felt, and the next phase of exponential growth is emerging in the blockchain sector.

It seems quite likely that the next phase of the digital revolution will be all about the blockchain. Exponential growth in blockchain adoption is now apparent simply because the blockchain may be the solution to a number of critical shortcomings that currently impede global commerce. These include critical factors such as the designation of trust in relationships and transactions, designation and verification of identity, verification of asset ownership, and the validation and recording of transactions. At present, all of these essential functions are operating in a sub-optimal way, but because the blockchain can enable radically expanded functionality in all of these areas it may well be the critical enabler of the next phase of economic transformation. The blockchain will enable radically expanded functionality through the adoption of new standards and technologies based on interlinking systems of distributed ledgers, de-centralized identity servers, verifiable claims, and trustable timestamping to address those deficiencies in a transformational manner. In its full realization, this will in essence be an entirely new platform, or infrastructure, to support all forms of commerce, both locally and globally.

Based on its expected advantages the blockchain is likely in position to become the fifth major disruptive computing paradigm in the history of the Information Age, following mainframes, PCs, the Internet, and mobile/social networking.

First disruption: Mainframes made it possible to manage global enterprises in new and much more efficient ways than were previously possible, which led to new scales of commerce that had previously been unattainable.

Second disruption: The PC of course extended these capabilities to individual users, leading to decentralized commerce and its radical expansion, and to the emergence of the creative economy.

Third disruption: The Internet helped to forge a global system of interconnected computer networks that use the Internet protocol suite (TCP/IP) to link devices worldwide. The changes driven by the Internet have had an enormous impact on the conduct of every aspect of our society, business, government, education and private life.

Fourth disruption: Interpersonal computing, the nexus of social and mobile capabilities, has extended the Internet revolution much deeper into personal life, extending the impact even more. From politics, to business, to cyberbullying and privacy, the reach of technology is now both pervasive and profound. It is also inexorable – we're not going back.

Each of these revolutions emerged through the intense and high-speed interactions among a large ecosystem of players and core technologies, the hardware platforms, the software architectures, the end user applications, and the service providers. So why do we think that a fifth revolution is now emerging? Clearly each new wave of technology has had immediate and enduring economic implications, and indeed each of these revolutions has altered and significantly expanded how and where we do business. Nevertheless, in the end all commerce is based on a few elusive and often intangible factors including trust, verification of identity, and undisputed ownership of assets. These are the essential infrastructure upon which all commerce depends, but in the omnidirectional, internet-enabled global marketplace, these factors are burdened by archaic approaches and an infrastructure well suited to industrialism, but not at all to the many ways we do commerce today, or the ways we inevitably will do it tomorrow. In other words, the emerging, digital-enabled, globalized economy is still burdened by critical deficiencies, and blockchains are attractive precisely because they can address every single one of these factors more effectively than previously possible.

This is the key blind spot to see beyond—just as the creators of Uber and Lyft realized that the taxi medallion system was archaic, and while nearly everyone assumed the existing taxi model was "the way things are," Uber and Lyft have proven that the ways things are isn't necessarily the way things will be.

The blockchain will have similarly profound impact because it's a technology for disrupting business models, one that is quite likely to disrupt markets far beyond bitcoin digital currency, which we see as its first "pilot" application but neither its last nor its most significant. Indeed, we anticipate that the blockchain will move from being seen as "programmable money" to become a preferred means of designating and validating programmable value, programmable governance, programmable contracts, programmable ownership, programmable trust, programmable identity, and programmable assets. As these elements constitute the essential foundations upon which commerce rely, what we're describing is nothing less than a fundamental revolution.

Hence, a "big bang" of innovation, development, and investment activity related to blockchains is now underway. The use of the blockchain in financial services and healthcare is significant, with firms including Citibank, NASDAQ and Goldman Sachs all investing in blockchain applications, and novel applications are being invented ranging from tamper-proof national voting systems, to pilots of blockchain-based music streaming services, to tracking blood diamonds, to a global framework for managing a decentralized Internet of Things.

If we study the structure of prior computing revolutions, we observe that the global acceleration of change has made it easier for each successive wave to achieve global penetration and impact more quickly than the previous, and so we foresee that the blockchain revolution will unfold at an even faster, seemingly breakneck speed. Hence, those who wait will be left behind. If you believe, as we do, that the blockchain revolution is real, then "wait-and-see" is probably not a success strategy. What's required is to approach the blockchain arena with clear vision, agility, and a seasoned team, so you are capable of recognizing and quickly seizing opportunities in this exponentially expanding market space.

This workbook presents practical methods and processes to help you prepare for this next wave of disruptive technology. The first step is learning a new vocabulary about blockchains and decentralized consensus, and the next step is to see how this may impact your business, business model and industry. The third step is to bravely leap into the next plot twist of the unfolding digital age by developing your own blockchain roadmap, to assure that your organization isn't left behind. And don't forget to have fun when you jump in!

BLOCK CHAIN

CHAPTER 1: BLOCKCHAINS WILL CHANGE THE WORLD

"The first generation of the digital revolution brought us the Internet. The second generation — powered by the blockchain — is bringing us a new platform to reshape the world of business."—Don Tapscott

THE BLOCKCHAIN IS POWERING A NEW wave of innovation that promises to change everything all over again. This digital tsunami is steadily building momentum, and it is predicted to disrupt virtually every business simply because it is itself a tool precisely useful for disrupting business models. It will thereby provoke a network effect of change, and thus we expect to see deeper and more profound levels of business disruption even than in previous waves.

The key underlying this technology shift is the adoption of immutable, decentralized ledgers that can reliably track and thus attest to virtually any form of ownership. Because this occurs without the need for any central government authority, blockchain is a force for the extension of borderless commerce and implies fundamental new means of exchange, which explains why the financial services industry is one of the first to engage in deep and widespread blockchain developments. But it's only the first.

Bitcoin, which uses the blockchain is its underlying technology, can be seen as a form of dress rehearsal for this new enabling technology, while the following waves will be all about who owns it and how people own property, money, content, identity, attention... Whatever can be owned can now be notated in free and open ledgers that validate ownership and thus facilitate exchange.

Ignoring the blockchain will thus be akin to saying, around 2000, "Do we really need a website?" or in 2008, "Isn't it safer to wait to see if this smartphone thing is for real to develop a mobile app?"

What is a Blockchain?

The first thing that we must understand at a deep level is just what these things are.

Here's my definition: a blockchain is a consensually validated multi-party database, or a public ledger, of all transactions or digital events that have been made between participating parties within a business eco-system.

That's certainly a mouthful so let me break down and explain what this means (although at a conceptual level, it's actually pretty simple).

Consider this analogy: If you and I were alone in a room, and I gave you $5, you could say later, "No you didn't!" and we would be deadlocked. Two voices with differing opinions, and no third party to validate one or the other. But if we were in a room with fifty people witnessing it (these are what we call "miners" in the bitcoin world) it becomes impractical to deny what happened. This is what programmers will call "a non-repudiatable transaction," and that's why it's "consensually validated." What we have is thus the equivalent of 50 cryptographic witnesses who attest that "it really did happen."

(By the way, if you gave 26 of those witnesses a dollar bribe to say "oh no he didn't," that's known as the "51% hack.")

While at a conceptual level it's simple, at the underlying technology level—the process of cryptographically insuring a transaction—it's genuinely a form of rocket science.

But let me ask you, does it really matter how it works? How many of us actually understand how a web server actually works? When the Web was young, we used plain old HTML 1.0, but nowadays it's a much more confusing myriad of technologies, including CSS, Javascript, web caching, blades, security, etc. But that doesn't stop you from using email, Wordpress or Mailchimp does it? Or from hiring a web designer?

Do you really understand how the central processor chip in your smartphone works? Probably not. But are you happy to use it the phone text your friends, take photos, call an Uber, watch videos, etc. etc.? Of course you are!

Just like gravity, which actually very few people deeply understand, what really matters is that it works, and it does so reliably. Blockchains are like that—the need to "understand" the technology diminishes once we gain familiarity with what it does. This is a natural process, and otherwise we'd all have to be computer scientists to survive in the modern world.

For the "what it does," you can think of blockchains as Google Docs on steroids. Add a few other features including distributed consensus, immutability, and deep anonymity, and the resulting system has the potential to revolutionize the digital commerce world by enabling a distributed consensus in which each and every online transaction involving digital assets, past and present, can be verified at any time in the present or future.

For the "what they're good for," we identify blockchain apps in three types or generations. The first generation applications focus on basic record keeping functionality, providing immutable, time-stamped journals or ledgers of events that occurred. They're obviously good for functions like payment systems and stock trading. A classic example is wire transfers using the correspondent banking network, which now cost about $30 to send, but with a blockchain they could become essentially free and instantaneous, thus becoming "Skype for money." We can also use blockchains in other ways, such as implementing unhackable elections and detecting black diamonds or counterfeit goods.

How important will all this become? Marc Andreessen, co-founder of Netscape and now a noted venture capitalist, recently declared the blockchain to be the most important invention since the Internet itself, while Johann Palychata of BNP Paribas wrote in the Quintessence magazine that the blockchain should be considered as an invention like the combustion engine that has the potential to transform the world of finance and beyond.

As we evolve toward more advanced forms of usage, other thought-provoking applications are possible. For example, a new kind of music distribution business would allow musicians to enjoy a more intimate connection with their fans and enable DJs to remix songs and share royalties automatically. If you buy Imogen Heap's song, "Tiny Human" with cryptocurrency you get the track's key, tempo, and stems. The money goes directly to the producers, writers, and engineers involved in the song's production, all split automatically without the need to audit the record label. (This automated revenue generation is an example of a "smart contract," which we'll get to shortly.)

This was a pilot test of a new music eco-system Heap envisioned called "Mycelia." It's more than just a payment platform, as it gives musicians absolute control over the data created by their songs as they circulate among fans and other musicians, including the song's credits, terms of usage dictated by the artist, where the song is played and when, and any transactions.

To understand the eventual power of this, think about the feedback listeners can provide directly, automated royalties generated by DJs remixing her work, and even perhaps bringing labels back into the eco-system to promote and market the works. But the most important fundamental impact is that the blockchain has become the innovation accelerator for the industry because it becomes the foundation of new ways that commerce can be organized. The emergence and spread of blockchains is thus a chance to deconstruct existing business models and rebuild them in new ways.

In practical terms, twenty years ago if a song sold a million copies the artist would receive about $45,000 in royalties and would win a platinum record. Today a major music service pays a pittance, about $35, for a million streams. The music industry desperately needs innovation, and the blockchain could deliver it.

We'll talk more about advanced blockchain functionality in both second and third generation applications in Chapter 11, but for now let's focus on second generation applications.

Dueling Blockchains

Blockchains will significantly reduce the cost of multi-party transactions, and even automate some contractual terms between then. They can this so because they essentially force an eco-system to accept a standardized data format, which will accelerate the adoption of open systems that unify and simplify a business eco-system.

At the same time, there's no reason that two different companies wouldn't compete by establishing two different blockchains, sort of like VHS vs Betamax, and fight it out in the market. This explains why so many firms are rushing to establish blockchains as soon as possible, why every major bank and stock exchange rushed to form a consortium to manage the deployment of blockchains... on their own terms —they each want to be first to market and establish an adoption lead.

This is also a bit like the Oklahoma land rush of 1889, when the state government opened two million acres to settlement. An estimated 50,000 people lined up to claim 160 acre plots. Of course, a number of the people entered the unoccupied land early and hid until the legal time of entry to lay quicker claim to more choice homesteads. They came to be known as "Sooners" and it's why Oklahoma is called "the Sooner State." So think of this book as your chance to become a "Blockchain Sooner."

Since competing blockchains will need to differentiate, and because blockchain technology is all about disrupting business models to remove middlemen and optimize processes, we are essentially entering a new battlefield of business model warfare. This workbook is also thus a strategy guide for building and tweaking business models, which tells us that it's also vital for you to understand the art and science of business model innovation. As we've repeatedly seen, the startups that win biggest are the ones with the best disruptive business models. Google, Facebook, Amazon, Uber, AirBNB, and many others achieved giga-scale growth by re-imagining the core business model of their industries, which tells us that engaging in Business Model Innovation isn't just a fanciful thought experiment, but a core requirement in the emerging marketplace of creative destruction.

How to Build a Successful Blockchain

Let's wrap this chapter up by summarizing why the blockchain space is so important. First, the web was really just another way to stay in touch with customers, albeit a powerful two-way channel. Blockchains are fundamentally something new; they are a way to innovate with business models, hence they are essentially a battlefield for business model warfare, and so this workbook is essentially a strategy guide for building and then refining new business models. Second, whoever deploys a blockchain for a particular industry first can often figure out and troubleshoot new and disruptive business models sooner than others who are waiting and watching. This is the power of pilots for accelerated learning. Third, once a particular eco-system has adopted a particular blockchain solution, that chain could provide access to everyone in the eco-system (given optimal rules of engagement for access), and could therefore drive dramatic reductions in that highly sought-after holy grail, the cost to acquire new customers. Fourth, a blockchain is also an appstore because once everyone agrees on standards for how data is managed, the smart contracts and other tools that operate over a blockchain could be marketed via a blockchain appstore function.

Why does that matter? When you realize that the iOS App Store is also an innovation accelerator that allows developers to spend less than $100,000 to create cute mobile games that generate a million dollars a day in revenues, you also recognize that blockchains are precursors of a new kind of appstore for distributed social and business applications.

Fifth, it needs to be remembered that blockchains are created and maintained through the cooperation of a community, so to succeed you need to play well with partners. Knowing what true collaboration and partnership means, and what the limits are, is essential. And yet you also need to move quickly so that potential competitors feel that you have too much of a head start to try to compete.

A further benefit is that your blockchain can exist independently of established authorities or middlemen, which in the blockchain developer community they refer to as "self-sovereignty," and it is significant because it enables transactions to take place and be recorded outside of traditional governmental frameworks. Removing the government as a middle man could even facilitate more efficient and sometimes even safer transactions, and for this reason the United Nations is reportedly studying the use of blockchain-based identity documents in refugee camps, where governmental identity systems have collapsed, or where a national ID card could endanger family members back home.

Sixth, the use of a blockchain can enable people to manage a new kind of "trust" in varying degrees, thus facilitating much more nuanced sharing of information and metrics. This is significant because in the past trust was binary – either one did or did not trust the counterpart. Successful transactions therefore depended on absolute trust, or the willingness to take significant risks. With blockchains, however, trust is now a manageable variable and it can be modulated in different situations, which facilitates a much broader spectrum of collaborations and thus enables much more nuanced transactions.

Exercises for Chapter I: Background

1) In your industry, who is the core user in the mainstream of your market?
Identify three top characteristics of this user.

2) In your industry, what is the current dominant business model?
Identify three top characteristics of this model.

3) Jot down some of the ideas you already have for blockchains.

4) *What are some questions you have about blockchains?*

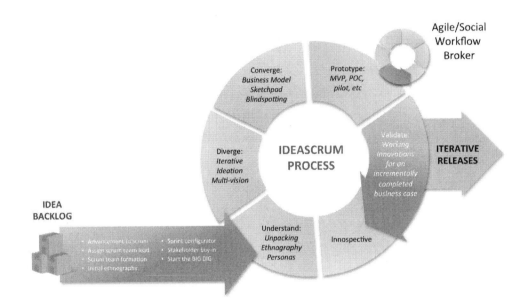

CHAPTER 2: PRINCIPLES OF AGILE INNOVATION

"At its root, Scrum is based on a simple idea: whenever you start a project, why not regularly check in, see if what you're doing is heading in the right direction, and if it's actually what people want?" —Jeff Sutherland

THE AGILE MOVEMENT WAS STARTED IN 2001 by a group of 12 programmers who felt intense frustration at the inadequacy of the prevailing approaches to large programming projects. Millions and millions of dollars were being wasted in failed technology projects. These horrors included some staggering, multi-billion dollar mega-failures that were truly monumental. Their goal was to address the productivity crisis in computer programming directly.

Fred Brooks coined the term "Brooks' Law" in 1975 in his seminal book, The Mythical Man-Month. Put simply, Brooks' Law states, "adding manpower to a late software project will only further delay the schedule and complete the project even later." This has been proven in study after study, so how do you deal with the chronic problem of late software? How do you get lean and mean, and ship software on time, on budget, and with a feature set that will continuously satisfy the evolving customer?

This was the problem that the founders of the Agile movement set out to address. The group was founded by senior programmers and project managers who were fed up with the status quo, and who felt there just had to be a better way. Not finding one ready at hand, they invented it. This approach they called "Agile" and it became their overarching philosophy, and was based on predecessors such as lean, quality, and re-engineering, all of which were powerful management techniques that lead to incremental improvements.

In their determination to develop and articulate a better way they wrote a simple document entitled "The Manifesto for Agile Software Development."

It was comprised of four simple (but also not so simple) statements:

We are uncovering better ways of developing software by doing it and helping others do it. Through this work, we have come to value:

1. *Individuals and interactions over processes and tools*
2. *Working software over comprehensive documentation*
3. *Customer collaboration over contract negotiation*
4. *Responding to change over following a plan*

Since Agile was invented specifically to address software programming projects, you might logically infer that its principles and practices are useful only or primarily in technology, but in fact the relevance of Agile is much broader. It has proven to be so brilliantly simple a way to organize people to get useful work done that its use is rapidly spreading beyond software into many other creative realms. Its insights and methods are applicable to nearly every kind of complex project that involves creativity and uncertainty, and hence it is legitimately the core of an approach that is proving to be nearly universal.

As a result, Agile is being used everywhere today, and for a very good reason: it actually works. It's used by companies like Apple, Alibaba, Google, Facebook and Tesla. The new values, principles, practices, and benefits are a radical alternative to command-and-control-style management. National Public Radio employs Agile methods to create new programming. John Deere uses them to develop new machines, and Saab to produce new fighter jets. C.H. Robinson, a global third-party logistics provider, applies them in human resources. And GE relies on Agile technique to transition itself from 20th-century conglomerate to 21st-century "digital industrial company." By taking people out of their functional silos and putting them in self-managed and customer-focused multidisciplinary teams, the Agile approach is not only increasing productivity, but also helping to train the next generation of corporate leaders.

Doing Agile

So how do you do Agile exactly? The fundamentals are pretty simple. To tackle an opportunity, the organization forms and empowers a small team, usually three to nine people, most of whom are assigned full-time. The team is cross-functional and includes all the skills necessary to complete its tasks. It manages itself and is strictly accountable for every aspect of the work. It uses a timeboxed and iterative approach, and consistently delivers something "working" and presentable at every iteration.

As Agile guru Jeff Sutherland explains, "Scrum doesn't have project managers. Instead, the team is empowered. They're responsible for the outcome, and they can manage themselves. The classic project manager 'boss' of the team isn't needed in Scrum. The team plans each Sprint based on the priorities of the Product Owner. They divide the work among themselves, make progress transparent and monitor themselves."

Thus, the team's product owner is ultimately responsible for delivering value to customers and users. The person in this role usually comes from a business function and divides his or her time between working with the team and coordinating with key stakeholders: customers, senior executives, and business managers. The product owner may use a technique such as design thinking or crowdsourcing to build a comprehensive "portfolio backlog" of promising opportunities. Then he or she continually and ruthlessly rank-orders that list according to the latest estimates of value to internal or external customers and to the company.

The product owner doesn't tell the team who should do what or how long tasks will take. Rather, the team creates a very simple road map and plans in detail only those activities that won't change during a reasonably tight window. Its members break the highest-ranked tasks into smaller modules, decide how much work the team will take on and how to accomplish it, develop a clear definition of "done," and then start building working versions of the product in short cycles (less than a month) known as sprints. A process facilitator, also called a scrum master, guides the process. This person protects the team from distractions and helps it put its collective intelligence to work.

This process is transparent to everyone, from team members to customers to management. No hiding or covering your ass. Team members hold brief daily "stand-up" meetings to review progress and identify roadblocks. They resolve disagreements through experimentation and feedback rather than endless debates or appeals to authority. They test small working prototypes of part or all of the offering with a few customers for short periods of time. If customers get excited, a prototype may be released immediately, even if some senior executive isn't a fan, or others think it needs more bells and whistles. The team then brainstorms ways to improve future cycles and prepares to attack the next top priority.

And that's all there is to it.

Combining Agile and Innovation

How do you blend the Agile with the innovation? Excellent question! The merger of Agile and Innovation can be understood by this simple formula:

Ideation + Execution = Innovation

The point, obviously, is that while ideation and execution may once have been seen as opposites, they're really synergistic complements. Without execution, ideation yields just a bunch of ideas that never go anywhere. Without ideation, execution is a fruitless exercise of re-arranging the deck chairs on the way to the rendezvous with an iceberg. Agile Innovation is the techniques and methodologies for both empowering and integrating ideation and execution.

To pull it off, you need to involve nearly every aspect of the organization, from the executive boardroom to the front line, to the back office and the development labs. Its goal, ultimately, is to enable the real-time enterprise of the 21st century. The process is meant to provide the fuel needed to inspire the entire engine of the enterprise.

At the same time that Agile was coming into being, the innovation movement was also evolving, developing and integrating methodologies like scenario planning, six sigma, linear innovation, actor-network theory, roadmapping, co-creation, reverse innovation, triz, open innovation, and most recently, design thinking. All of these disciplines and techniques are pre-cursors and ingredients for the Agile Innovation approach.

The key function of both Agile and innovation is that each process is performed in deep collaboration with users and/or customers, so the team receives immensely valuable feedback directly from actual end users who are working collaboratively with them on a day to day basis. This process optimizes learning about the underlying or targeted value proposition, while conversely unpleasant surprises are reduced or eliminated altogether. No participant of an Agile project was ever "shocked and dismayed" by the final results because they were right there with the team, step by step, co-designing, reviewing the results step by step, providing mid-course corrective feedback, and co-owning the results. This is, obviously, a formula for successful co-design and collaboration. And in the next chapter, we'll show exactly how Agile and Innovation are blended into the Agile Innovation Design Sprint.

The Agile Sprint

Agile projects are organized into multi-week sprints during which specific deliverables are planned and expected to be accomplished, and the work is managed accordingly. If you're a software developers, much of this might feel familiar.

The basic diagram that depicts the 1 – 4 week sprint process:

1. The Product Backlog is the master list of all the work that is to be done. This list is developed at the very outset of a project, and reflects the team's design for their work.

2. The Sprint Backlog is the targeted list of the team's immediate work. It is carefully selected by the project management team to be successfully addressable by the size of the team, and by the duration of time that is allotted.

3. The 2 – 4 Week Sprint Cycle is the interval over which work is accomplished.

4. The 24-hour Scrum Cycle is how work gets done on a daily basis.

5. The Daily Scrum Meeting is how the team maintains alignment throughout the Sprint. This short meeting is typically about 10 minutes long and it's done standing up, so no one is tempted to lean back in their chairs and prolong a quick update into a time-wasting gab fest.

6. The Results are completed work, incremental results that are assessed against goals, and of course assessed from the customer's perspective, to determine the degree to which they meet or exceed expectations. After the assessment, the Product Backlog is then revised as needed, and a new sprint is initiated.

These elements are central to the implementation of Agile Software methodology and its goal of delivering working code, and the same elements are also hugely useful in helping innovation teams to work effectively and to meet the primary goal of Agile Innovation, which is delivering working and market-moving innovations in the least possible time. This approach is obviously designed to optimize meaningful progress, and since the Product Backlog can be revised at any time based on new information or due to changing external factors, this is a system that also responds to change.

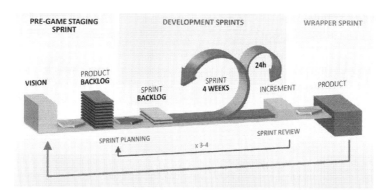

FIGURE 1: THE SCRUM CYCLE

Adapting the Agile Manifesto

Agile has twelve principles, and we've adapted them to address innovation:

Agile Manifesto Principles	Agile Innovation Principles
1. Our highest priority is to satisfy the customer through early and continuous delivery of valuable software.	1. Delight the customer through rapid delivery of a minimal key feature set
2. Welcome changing requirements, even late in development. Agile processes harness change for the customer's competitive advantage.	2. Welcome changing requirements by building in a rapid pivot innovation model
3. Deliver working software frequently, from a couple of weeks to a couple of months, with a preference to the shorter timescale.	3. Deliver value continuously that address progressively deeper tacit customer needs
4. Business people and developers must work together daily throughout the project.	4. Agile innovation is a team sport, implemented on a daily basis
5. Build projects around motivated individuals. Give them the environment and support they need, and trust them to get the job done.	5. Build projects around incented and empowered innovators
6. The most efficient and effective method of conveying information to and within a development team is face-to-face conversation.	6. Convey information face-to-face using a co-facilitation process
7. Working software is the primary measure of progress.	7. Working innovations are the primary measure of progress
8. Agile processes promote sustainable development. The sponsors, developers, and users should be able to maintain a constant pace indefinitely.	8. Maintain a consistent cadence of progress by adopting a proven methodology
9. Continuous attention to technical excellence and good design enhances agility.	9. Aim to simultaneously master customer insight and technical excellence
10. Simplicity – the art of maximizing the amount of work not done – is essential.	10. Simplicity is essential
11. The best architectures, requirements, and designs emerge from self-organizing teams.	11. Unleash your ideation by unlocking your team's core creativity
12. At regular intervals, the team reflects on how to become more effective, then tunes and adjusts its behavior accordingly.	12. Teams should hold innospectives to continuously learn and improve

TABLE 1: AGILE MANIFESTO ADAPTATION

Exercises for Chapter 2: Agile Innovation

1) Has your organization implemented Agile? If so, how do you do it?

2) Has your company implemented a formal innovation process? If so, what are you doing?

Phase **1** **2** **3** **4** **5** **6**

understand

- PAINstorming
- User personas
- Ethnography
- Needsfinding
- Stakeholders

diverge

- Ideate
- Multi-vision
- Think visual
- Reframe
- Unleash

converge

- BizModel Canvas
- Pain acuteness
- Blindspots
- Find the spine
- First five steps

prototype

- Find the MVP
- User test script
- Prototype fidelity
- Find the tool
- Timebox it

validate

- Panorama
- The BIG vision
- Happily ever after
- Meet cute
- The throughline

innospective

- Three words
- Happy about
- Needs work
- Ideate the process
- Share the ideas

CHAPTER 3:
HOW TO DO A DESIGN SPRINT

"The Design Sprint has proven to be the most effective way to increase the chance of a business to succeed."—Sergio Panagìa

FOR THIS PARTICULAR EXERCISE OF DESIGNING a blockchain and its associated business model, Agile innovation can be tactically implemented via a design sprint. A design sprint is a structured process of taking an idea from initial design concept through refinement, prototyping and user testing. The structure of the process guides innovation teams by helping people break out of limited or linear thinking, to focus and discover what really works and what really matters: the perspectives of the users. It thus orients the teams around the value of an idea by putting the end user's perspective at the core of the innovation effort, and aligns everyone on the team to the goal of hitting the target cleanly.

Our approach to an Agile Design Sprint is executed in six phases:

Understand

Diverge

Converge

Prototype

Validate

Innospective

The design sprint process is quite popular now, and used in a growing number of Silicon Valley companies including Google Ventures, Nest and others. Design sprints at Google are often 5-day intensive events akin to an extended hackathon, but our approach is a bit more malleable, and we sometimes call it an adaptive design sprint because it can be configured for any suitable time frame, based on the awareness that many innovation projects simply can't be stuffed into a five day time window, especially considering the prototyping stages in hardware and biotech. In addition, sometimes people with full time roles who are valuable contributors simply cannot contribute full-time over the course of a comprehensive design effort.

Also, frankly, when a venture capitalist does a design sprint, the unspoken reality is that they really want to "get to a no faster" most of the time, i.e., filter out the weaker companies faster. If this is your baby, you will want to take the time to do the best job you can, with the focus on improvement rather than filtering. Again, the VC really only cares about the one in twenty with unicorn potential, and not like a third grade teacher who vows to leave no child behind.

Fundamentally, the design sprint is implemented in six steps:

Phase I: Understand

To invent great new products and services you'll have to see the world differently. That is, you'll have to see what could be rather than what merely is, so you can never be contented and satisfied with the current state of knowledge and practice. Based on this concept it's obvious that you'll also have to change the way you look and thus the way you see in order to see differently, which means you'll also have to change the way you think.

Further, since what we did and what we've got isn't going to cut it in the era of exponential change and hyper-competition, we are compelled to find the critical differences. Hence, for that we must understand the future, and the means to doing so is to continuously expand our methods of perception. Consequently, the initial phase of the design sprint is perceptual: using a wide range of observation tools to gain a profound understanding of the needs of users and customers.

Leading marketing practitioners and product designers know this already. They know that it's mandatory to study user behavior and user needs quite deeply before leaping into the product design process, and the intensity of required study has increased with the increasing sophistication of both the products (technology) and of the customers (ever more enabled and engaged). Many leaders are applying advanced methods of "design ethnography"

and "observational field work" to expose these needs, focusing particularly on detecting unarticulated needs on which to build breakthrough products. These are also referred to as "tacit" needs, meaning that while they are present, they are usually unspoken. Frequently those experiencing them (a customer, typically) is not consciously aware that this dimension of their own experience is even occurring, and so it's up to the observer to discover what's going on, and what could be better.

The intent is to decode unspoken needs and expectations, and thus the first part of understanding is collecting relevant observations. This is not done in a laboratory setting, but in real life situations where people are engaged in their day to day activities.

The second part of the understanding process is to figuring out what it is that the team actually observed. We call this "unpacking," a term used in clinical psychology which means carefully sorting and distinguishing the rich complexity in emotional experiences. Recognizing and understanding those emotional forces and energies is vital for understanding tacit needs that can become the basis of great designs.

During the unpacking process, team members present and discuss their observations and impressions, and through discussion they seek a shared understanding of the research findings and priorities. These they then translate into "problem statements."

Problem statements are concise expressions of the needs and goals of customers – both conscious and unconscious – which must then be translated into new ideas for the design of products, services, and business models.

Phase II: Divergence

Problem statements are the basis from which a team can begin generating solution ideas, a divergent process of exploring what could be done across a very wide field of possibilities. This is classically known as "brainstorming," but that's just one of a great many approaches that could be fruitful here.

We also know that great innovations are often stimulated less with a focus on coming up with the right answers, and more by asking the right questions. Great questions are "ideation lenses" or "innovation perspectives" that boldly illuminate the challenges, problems, shortcomings, and needs, and goals. And when these have been nicely illuminated the ideas tend to flow readily behind.

To stimulate the formation of great questions we apply the process called multi-visioning, during which we adopt a particular perspective for inquiry for a short amount time, perhaps 10 – 15 minutes and then shift the perspective through a series of structured tangents.

In multiple iterations we sample a variety of perspectives and engage in coming up with ideas from only that perspective. This embeds an iterative process with time-boxing – setting a time limit for each perspective – which allows a team to very effectively diverge and generate a lot of promising ideas faster. Facilitation can guide teams to identify multiple directions that will most likely bear fruit.

Divergence results in a vast inventory of possibilities. Very often these are recorded as Post-it notes on the wall, taking advantage of a large surface where a wide range of ideas can be viewed and assessed at a single glance.

Phase III: Convergence

The purpose of divergence is to come up with a very large number of very good ideas. It's followed by convergence, which is when we identify the spine of the story we're seeking to tell, the central core of the innovation narrative that explains who the customers are and how we are creating unique value for them. Focusing and narrowing the design to the most viable solution or solutions helps the team to figure out what needs to be built, tested and validated.

We might look for this spine by using clustering and multi-voting techniques to identify which directions are most promising, and thus to pull out the key elements of the narrative. We can cluster ideas by moving Post-it notes to gather similar themes into related themes and topics, which often then forms the spine itself. Multi-voting with sticky dots is another approach that gives a voice to each team member, and ensures that more forceful speakers cannot dominate the conversation.

At this point we may find convergence on a single idea and story spine, or we may have identified a few major alternative possibilities that we need to explore in more depth in order to arrive at the one that best crystalizes our intent and best realizes the maximum value.

Similarly, the spine of an innovation story is not just the core feature set or the "minimal viable product," but the meaning of both the core feature set as part of the overall vision that connects with the user at an emotional level. Entrepreneurs must only understand not only what their invention/innovation does at a functional level, they should also strive to understand why it matters. This is why I included the "Start with Why" story in the first chapter.

This links the user's objectives together into a thread, and pushes the underlying concept forward to the expression of its meaning. Hence, we focus not only on the what, but equally or even more importantly, on the why. The throughline thus acts as a compass, guiding the direction in which the energy of the innovation team will flow constructively.

Phase IV: Prototyping

The fourth stage is Prototyping, the process of transforming ideas into real, usable elements and artifacts that can be seen, held, and used. Nothing is more compelling than a good working prototype, which appeases even the most wary and pragmatic stakeholder, because they, too, can then see for themselves. It's easy to imagine the prototype of a car or a phone and to understand how important is to make such a prototype in the process of designing such complex technologies. Creating such a prototype enables us to see if all the pieces really do fit together as intended. Architects also make prototypes, although they generally call them "models," and of course the model of a house or skyscraper is usually smaller than the eventual house or skyscraper.

Planning projects also produce prototypes, although we're more likely to call them "drafts." Normally we'll prepare a first draft and circulate it among our team to get everyone's inputs and corrections before moving on to a more defined "second draft," and even perhaps a third draft before finalizing. Hence, chances are that every form of prototype will become part of a family, as we'll create not just a single prototype, but a series of them, each more refined than the previous, as we converge toward a final design.

Engaging in these prototyping iterations means that we are going through stages of progressive validation, which is what we do when we test our prototype, or edit the draft of our document, or build a second and third model. Each subsequent version reveals to us additional details and nuances that enable to us move progressively toward a final version that meets all of the requirements that we identified in the understanding stage.

The additional value of prototyping lies not just in its persuasive value, but in the fact that a working prototype validates an underlying concept by making it actually work. Hence, in this phase the team fleshes out their design to a level of detail sufficient to validate the core design direction.

Prototypes are thus a way to formulate better questions, and having the right questions is the heart of the path to optimizing the design. Consequently, some areas of a prototype, those that correspond to what you want validated sooner, may need to be more detailed than the rest of the prototype. We refer to this as high fidelity vs. low fidelity prototyping, and a typical prototype will combine high and low fidelity elements as required by the logic of what needs to be demonstrated to gain the required knowledge.

The level of fidelity will also be based on how many iterations you've been through. For a first iteration, especially a v1.0 design sprint with only a day to build a prototype, it's obviously expected that a conceptual mockup is the right output, which some call a "Powerpoint prototype."

Phase V: Validation

It's important to note that the fifth stage, Validation, requires real-world testing to assure that our prototype is as robust as it needs to be. Thus, we test not only in our highly controlled lab environment, but also in the field, with real users or customers, in real world environments that are often dirty, chaotic, and messy. You can also think of the loop between prototyping and validation as a way to ask progressively better questions, and then to find satisfying answers to them on the road to optimizing your design.

Often the validation phase includes interviews with users who are given hands on experiences with prototypes, following which we talk with them to learn what they experienced. It's important that they express their feelings in their own words, as it is often the subtle nuances of their experiences that will enable us to create results that are truly outstanding.

Validation is a reality check that determines exactly how far you've come, how far you still need to go, or if you need to pivot to a different approach. Hence, this is the flip side of the observational field work we did in Phase I, except now we do "validation ethnography." Whereas before we were looking for insights into the needs and expectations of customers, and particularly the unspoken ones, now we will circle back to some of those same customers and explore with them the value proposition that we have achieved through our prototypes.

Functionally, this means that you'll conduct a series of interviews with users as they use your prototype. Do they like it? Do they love it? Do they hate it? Do they understand it? Do they care?

The findings from this should not come as a surprise to you, as you've had customers participating in the scrum team all along, but it may nevertheless be revealing. And in any case the documented findings from these validations, assuming they are positive, will be very useful in soliciting further support for your work.

Experience suggests that all you need are five validation subjects to get a robust sampling of opinions, although you may need many more than this if the findings show a broad range of likes and dislikes.

Using ethnographic techniques, observe your end user actually using the prototype. Notice what makes sense and what doesn't, and then compile your notes about what you learned. Do your findings reinforce or conflict with your product theory? What are the additional stories and observations, the flow of interaction, the key learnings?

Phase VI: Innospective

And this brings us to the sixth and final stage of the agile design sprint, which we term "Innospective." This is where we turn our attention inward to consider how well we did through the previous five stages of the innovation process, and seek to learn how we could do better next time. Military organizations often undertake a comparable process called the "after action review," wherein the participants in a war game or an actual military engagement will discuss the process and the outcomes and seek to identify what's gone well and what must be improved for next time.

This is an essential component of the overall process to improve the capabilities of the team members, the performance of the organization, and the results that overall innovation process achieves. One of the key Agile principles states: At regular intervals, the team reflects on how to become more effective, then tunes and adjusts its behavior accordingly.

The entire team should participate in the innospective. Everyone should be encouraged to share their highs and lows, and to reflect on and share the lessons they have learned through the process. Were the tools adequate? Was communication within the team effective? What worked out exceptionally well? Where did we fall short of our own expectations?

The entire design sprint may be a process that lasts a day, or a week, or a few weeks, and by rigorously following the six stages it enables us to not only produce outstanding results, but to simultaneously build our capacity to do even better next time, because we are intentionally learning how to do it better through a focused effort of reflection and discussion.

The entire sprint may be a process that lasts a week, or a few weeks, and by rigorously following the six stages it enables us to not only produce outstanding results, but to simultaneously build our capacity to do even better next time, because we are intentionally learning how to do it better through a focused effort of reflection and discussion.

Exercises for Chapter 3: Design Sprint

1) In your industry, what is the current dominant business model?
Identify three top characteristics of this model.

2) *If you already know how to do a design sprint, come up with some ways to improve it.*

CHAPTER 4: BLOCKCHAIN DEEP DIVE

"I think the fact that within the bitcoin universe an algorithm replaces the functions of government… is actually pretty cool. I am a big fan." –Al Gore, 45th Vice President of the United States

L ET'S TALK ABOUT WHAT MAKES BLOCKCHAINS tick, so that we can learn about how you can make one work for you. Blockchains are actually pretty simple. A blockchain is a place on the web where you store data, via what computer scientists call a "linear data container space" (ie, the block), in a "partially public" manner. The reason it's partially public is because anyone can verify that information in the block, but it's encrypted so only you know it's yours, and can prove it with private digital keys paired to that data. It's a bit like your home address: you can publish your home address publicly so it can be found, but that address doesn't give any information about what your home looks like on the inside, or what property it contains. You'll need your private key to enter your private home, and since you have claimed that address as yours, no one else can claim the same address as theirs. Thus, it's based on public visibility, but private inspection. Make sense?

Hence, the blockchain behaves almost like a database, with the additional feature that it has embedded rules about who can see what. This means that you don't need a bank, or an escrow agent, or a government, or any other middle men, to make it happen.

(Or to demand a cut.) The content you're storing can about anything digital, as well as tokens of value or a cryptographically protected money balance. Hence the blockchain acts as an alternative value transfer system that no central authority—nor malicious third party—can tamper with.

Three additional concepts are central to the blockchain computing paradigm and also provide opportunities for better addressing business models: (a) decentralized consensus, (b) trust computing, and (c) smart contracts.

There are a number of other conceptsthat are internal to the system, like "proof of work"—a system that prevents users from changing records on the blockchain without re-doing a lot of work unwinding previous transactions, or "Merkle trees"—that power the cryptographic functionality. But these are not germane to how you, as a business manager, can take advantage of the technology at the application level.

Decentralized Consensus

The world up to now has been run on centralized consensus—i.e., a single, central database rules all, and through this, authority can also centralize. The emerging model for how the world will be run is de-centralized, and that will have an effect on centralized authority. What the blockchain protocol does essentially, is transfer authority and trust to decentralized virtual networks, and enables their nodes to continuously and sequentially record transactions on a public "block."

What's important here is that with the use of blockchains, the middle man can be removed from how business works. Therefore, applications can be written to be organically decentralized, and that is the spark that will drive a myriad of business model innovations.

A tremendous variety of transaction types could be affected: escrow transactions, bonded contracts, third party arbitration, multiparty signatures, and any entity that provide registrations, tickets, certificates and rights and obligations in real estate, cars, art works and so on. It will eventually include every market and every imaginable asset type, physical or digital. What we are seeing now is a transition from Bitcoin as a decentralized asset tracking system to the blockchain as a decentralized programmable trust infrastructure.

So the goal is for you to analyze and fully understand how blockchains might make your business sector more decentralized. How does authority work? How can you shift the locus of authority back to the participants of your eco-system? How are transactions secured or settled? Who are the middle men, and how could you dis-intermediate them? How can you reduce costs or increase functionality by moving to the blockchain?

Trust computing

For blockchains to work, we must enable computers to trust one another at a deeper level. In the past, institutions and central organizations were necessary as trusted authorities make things work, but now with the blockchain serving as a decentralized validator of transactions, each peer can proceed and trust one another because the rules of trust, compliance, authority, governance, contracts, law, and agreements—which are built into the technology rather than embedded in institutional trust authorities. This is a fundamental shift, leading to the transformation of trust from individuals and institutions to low cost, automated and self-managing systems.

So how is that trust generated exactly? For example, the accessibility of the source code that supports the blockchain eco-system creates trust in the system, as everyone can see how the code is written. All users of the blockchain can thus verify for themselves that the underlying code has no security flaws or contains no back doors that permit tampering. Openness and transparency builds trust in the system. Plus, the generated ledger is built with a consensus-driven distributed database structure. But does it go deeper than the technology?

The flip side of trust is transparency. The blockchain's approach to transparency allows all users to check that their copy of the ledger is consistent with all other users' copies, while maintaining their confidentiality. In programmer speak, any well-connected node is able to determine, with reasonable certainty, whether a transaction does or does not exist in its data set. Any node that creates a transaction can, after a confirmation period, determine with a reasonable level of certainty whether the transaction is valid, able to take place and become final, i.e. that no conflicting transactions were confirmed into the blockchain elsewhere that would invalidate the transaction. In the Bitcoin world, this is called the double spending problem.

This level of transparency, however, may in some cases, become a challenge for the privacy of its user. The Bitcoin network strives to preserve the privacy of its users by allowing nodes to access the ledger under a pseudonym. This would be problematic in the traditional business world. As mentioned before, the entity transferring a Bitcoin to the node does not have to reveal the physical identity of the person or organization operating the node. All that is needed is that the node makes the transaction with a digital signature with a valid private cryptographic key. If the use of a blockchain 2.0 application demands a link to a user's identity, this personal information will need to be made accessible for those who use the application.

This creates challenges in respect of compliance with something like the European Union's data protection regulation. Some of these challenges are similar to those faced by international e-commerce websites. Others may be new. If a blockchain database holds personal data in clear text, this information will be copied on all distributed copies of the ledger to all nodes. Who are these nodes? In an EU data protection context, who are data controllers and data processors? These should be viewed as opportunities for developing solutions that provide better blockchain solutions for your market sector, and its vagaries around trust and identity.

Smart Contracts

Smart contracts are little programs that you can entrust with a unit of value (such as a cyber-token or some money), along some rules about what to do in order to fulfill the terms and conditions of the contract. Many kinds of contractual clauses may thus be made partially or fully self- executing. The big idea here is that a transaction's contractual governance between two or more parties could now be verified programmatically via the blockchain, instead of via a central arbitrator or governmental authority.

The thinking goes like this: why depend on a central authority when two or more parties can agree between themselves, and have the software fulfill the agreement programmatically? Thus, the parties define and agree on the "programmatically actionable" rules, and embed them inside the transactions, enabling an end-to-end resolution to be self-managed between computers that represent the interests of the users. By integrating smart contract technology, blockchains can enable contracts at a significantly lower cost, and enable all sorts of new possibilities.

The concept of the smart contract was first proposed in 1994 by a programmer named Nick Szabo, who had the idea to automatically execute contracts between participating parties, triggered by changes in the database and in trustable events outside the database. However, this concept did not find usage until the notion of crypto currencies with programmable payments came into existence. This is similar to what banks offer with "auto-pay" that automatically pay your monthly mortgage for you, except in this case, it's something like when a ship's GPS indicates that it's passed the halfway point between departing and destination ports.

The underlying hypothesis is that once the terms and conditions are set in computer code, the contract should be automatically executed, self-enforcing, and impartial. In many commercial relationships, in particular within financial services, these properties make smart contracts very attractive, and will significantly decrease transaction costs.

Thinking farther into the future, theoretically, the inclusion of programmable actions could turn contracts in "smart contracts," property in "smart property," and money into "smart money"—imagine the power of money that is fundamentally "unstealable," and property that recognizes it rightful owner. Many blockchain pundits believe that Smart Contracts are the killer app the blockchain and cryptocurrency world. Smart contracts can facilitate, verify or enforce the negotiation of contracts and eliminate the need for a physical document. They eliminates the need for an intermediary, such as a broker, exchange, bank or escrow company.

Why should this be meaningful to you, as a prospective blockchain developer? Because optimizing trust is one way to provide differentiated services, and better monetize blockchain technology in your industry. So from a technical viewpoint, if you can do it better than a competitive blockchain solution provider can - you can provide a superior solution that delivers a competitive advantage.

Are Smart Contracts Actually Legal?

This is a good question. Legally speaking, for an agreement to be enforceable or recognizable at law, there needs to be an offer, an acceptance of those terms, and a mutual exchange of value or consideration. Thus, single sided "smart contracts" are probably not enforceable. Also, the legal system generally offers remedies for the breach of a legally binding agreement, such as a requirement to pay damages, so these need to be included.

Per this working definition proposed above, many attorneys believe that smart contracts are probably legally binding, provided that execution of the agreement (the signing) is via a legally accepted manner. Nick Szabo's posited that a vending machine transaction is essentially a smart contract, consistent with the working definition: insert a dollar and you get a can of soda. Now in the case of this vending machine transaction, there actually is a legally binding contract behind it. Inserting a buck constitutes acceptance. The soda pop is consideration. And if the machine eats my dollar without giving me a soda, I would have legal recourse. Actually, there are already plenty of examples of smart contracts, like adjustable-rate mortgage, bill auto-pay, sweep accounts, and so on.

Unintended Consequences

The upside of smart contracts definitely sounds rosy, but it should be noted that they offer both opportunity and complexity. If you want an analogy, think of ERP, aka enterprise resource planning, which is the use of a system of integrated software applications to manage a business and automate its back office functions related to technology, services and human resources. It's sort of like smart contracts, but inside of a company.

Now, the important thing to remember is that according to the analyst firm Gartner, approximately 75 percent of all ERP projects fail, at some level. That is a very sobering statistic, especially when you consider that a major ERP implementation could cost upwards of $40-50 million. And most usually run late, go way over-budget, and simply do not deliver anywhere near the planned results.

Smart contracts are even more complex than ERP system because they work between companies instead of inside them. At least inside a company, everyone won't be tempted to sue each other when the software starts misbehaving.

The point is this: as anyone who as actually signed a contract before, it's important to read the fine print. For any smart contract programming beyond a simplistic rule set, there will be bugs. When things go wrong, how do you handle unforeseen circumstances and resolve them? Provisions for handling programmatic errors and unintended consequences need to be explicitly defined in the contract terms.

Consider this example: the software looked fine and was even quite simple so everyone could agree the source code was correct... but there was a "compiler error" that made a mistake and had you overpay the other party? How do you fix that? Can you charge interest on the over-payment? What if some hacker caused the compiler error to send the tiny overpayment to his own account? Since there's no "centralized authority" that you're paying taxes to, why should the cyber-crime division any government pay to catch that hacker?

This is complicated stuff. Trying to cover every possible commercial agreement will be difficult, as contracts can become very complex. Drafting a legal contract needs to take into account all possible contingencies, and this is an area where considerable research and innovation will occur.

First, we need to consider the issue of the legal status of smart contracts. In other words, are they legally recognizable? The working definition of a "smart contract" is "a consensual arrangement between at least two parties for an automated, independent commercial result from the satisfaction or non-satisfaction, determined objectively through code, of a specific factual condition."

Smart Contract Technology

As this is a key blockchain functionality, with the greatest opportunity for customized solutions, let's continue diving deeper into the topic. Blockchain technology companies are already beginning to explore this new legal territory, by enabling smart contracts for blockchains. Many companies have begun to support them on an experimental basis, since much of the code is still in test mode and not yet approved and validated.

Again, the idea is that assets are transferred only after meeting certain conditions, for example, on acceptance of delivery, or completion of a milestone, or replacing or augmenting an escrow service. In particular, Ethereum has created a lot of excitement for its programmable platform capabilities. The company allows anyone to create their own cryptocurrency and use that to execute and pay for smart contracts, while it also possesses its own cryptocurrency (known as "ether") which is used to pay for the services. Ethereum is already powering a wide range of early applications in areas such as governance, autonomous banks, keyless access, ICO's, financial derivatives trading and settlement—all by using smart contracts.

Another solution comes from a company called Tezos, which offers a more advanced approach to smart contracts. While all blockchains offer financial incentives for maintaining consensus on their ledgers, no blockchain has a robust mechanism to seamlessly amend the rules governing its protocol and explicitly fund protocol development. Tezos takes a different approach by creating certain governance rules for stakeholders to approve of protocol upgrades that are then automatically deployed on the network. So when a developer proposes a protocol upgrade, they can attach an invoice to be paid out to their address upon approval and inclusion of their upgrade. This approach provides an incentive to contribute active thinking towards core development of the Tezos blockchain and further decentralizes the maintenance of the network.

The result is that it compensates developers for serious work with tokens that have immediate value, rather than forcing them to seek corporate sponsorships, foundation salaries, or work solely because "they're making the world a better place." Tezos can also insure that key properties are upheld over time, by providing something called "formal verification" for the software. This process of verifying a complex piece of software is a significant task, so the Tezos sought to simplify it by adopting a programming language called OCaml, which is very good at pattern matching and higher-order logic, and removes any ambiguity as to what is the intended behavior of financially weighted smart contract modules. In other words, this means that someone would be able to write rigorous mathematical proofs and have the computer system check that your program conforms to those proofs.

Say you had a multi-signature wallet contract and you want to have a rule that any single participant can withdraw up to some limit amount or a percentage of the funds per day, whichever is greater, but it requires two or three signatures to exceed that limit or withdraw all funds. With Ethereum smart contracts you write the code and then you pray that your code doesn't have a bug in it, or even if it's flawless code, there could be a "compiler error" that could be taken advantage of.

The downside with formal verification is that progress will be slow starting out, because there aren't a lot of programmers familiar with OCaml and mathematical proofs that could result in the loss of funds or very clever hacking. So there's a tradeoff between Ethereum and Tezos... if you want to be first to market you probably need to go with Ethereum, and aim to use only a very simple contract that is easily verified. Complexity is not your friend here. But if you require complex contract terms, and need rock solid proof that smart contracts will behave as promised, then Tezos will be superior.

Tezos therefore intends to be a "future-proof "smart contract system, using a built-in consensus mechanism so its protocol can evolve, and incorporate new innovations over time, without the risk of "hard forks" splitting the market with different versions of your blockchain. In the long run, a collection of formally verified contracts, libraries and proofs will be developed for Tezos and other platforms, and offered via app stores, but for now, it's the wild west out there, and the wagon trail is only just now starting out.

Formal verification is only one solution in what promises to become a rapidly growing arena of contract law. For example, if there's a bug in the system, who's liable for damages? The software vendors will surely include shrinkwrap and clickthru agreements limiting their liability. If the code is right, but a compiler error causes one party to over or under pay on a contract, is that an "act of God?"

Adjudicating Smart Contracts

When circumstances have changed in a way not foreseen by the parties at the time of entering into the contract, the contract must either be re-negotiated or adjudicated. But maybe a cheaper and better way to deal with this is to automate the process of "refactoring" a contract in some way? For example, both parties might agree beforehand that a contract's enforcement should be made contingent upon certain principles or even computational processes, like tying something to the prime lending rate, if an adjustment is required. Also, it is almost a certainty that smart contracts in the future will have to rely on courts and arbitration. These potentialities are so complex that for the foreseeable future, it is likely that only simple transaction types will be fully converted to smart contracts, and the interface processes for adjudication will likely be first defined by the governing bodies that control the courts and provide the contractual law framework. Hence, a significant issue is to provide for limitations of liability for companies providing blockchain services, which will be a requirement if we hope to establish a new form of economic transaction in the fully digital economy.

Designing Blockchain Applications

Let's assume you run a business that is contemplating leveraging a blockchain play or want to start up a blockchain venture from scratch. Given the structure of the underlying technology, how do you go about designing a meaningful blockchain strategy? The answer can be determined by looking at how businesses can benefit from blockchains, and focusing on the core pain points and how business models will be disrupted. That is essentially the goal of this workbook, and we'll work toward that goal in the following chapters. Let's start with the benefits...

First, they can help small and medium sized businesses reduce paperwork and operational costs. In other words, this means needing to pay less to accountants, lawyers, and bureaucratic government agencies. Why? Because transactions over blockchains are self-auditing. They're sometimes called "triple entry accounting" for this reason. This is years away, but this reduction of red tape and inefficieny is going to happen eventually.

Second, you can remove middle men and the costs for their services. Blockchains can help improve your supply chain margins by automating the process tracking and approving things using a distributed ledger.

Third, next generation blockchains will eventually move toward a process we call "marketization," that could reduce customer acquisition costs. Because identity is decentralized, participants in a certain blockchain could announce willingness to be contacted with offers and referrals. Thus, blockchains have the potential to help improve your sales channels, or demand chains, by automating those processes and removing middle men, and thereby reduce advertising and sales costs.

Fourth, blockchains will make it possible for small businesses to raise capital more efficiently, from new forms of trustable crowdfunding via evolving ICOs, to new models for receivables factoring. There's a blockchain startup in New York called Fluent which is "tokenizing invoices" – that's a fancy way of saying what we described in benefit number two. In blockchain parlance, it means it prevents the invoice from being factored multiple times, like Springtime for Hitler in the Broadway play, The Producers – or "double-spent" in the Bitcoin world. And when a history of reliable payment is recorded, it becomes possible to more easily factor those receivables in that flow.

Let's review this model using a concrete example. Suppose you love motorcycles and collect classic bikes. You work on them during the weekend with your grease monkey daughter, who grew up to become a whiz kid software engineer. One fine summer day, after a ride, she says to you, "Hey, you know, it would be really easy to do a blockchain for motorcycles!" The initial idea is to create a digital system for managing motorcycle repair records. So when you buy a rusty used motorcyle to restore, along with some parts to restore them with, you can track the provenance of everything that goes into the bike. You can know their history, what worked, what didn't, who did the work, whatever. It's like being the first to rush into the Internet thing twenty years ago, to grab a domain name like "dirtbikes.com." But it's more than just a digital land grab, because you get to organize the sharing of data, how people interested in a motorcyle culture will connect ot it, establishing ways to work with third parties like insurance companies, modernizing supply chain practices, and offering a bevy of trust and reputation services. What it delivers are lower costs, reduced risk, happier customers and more deeply connected partners in an emerging user-driven eco-system around motorcycles. If you do it right, it can lead to transformative revenue models and the dis-intermediation of middlemen, sort of like what Uber and AirBNB have done, but in an even bigger scale.

That's just for starters. Now let's add a few more things to the basket of benefits. Because of integration of blockchains with other technologies, the system can now mash up software from other developers more easily. So instead of just ordering parts from your regular vendor, someone can develop a system to automatically scan other reliable vendors to find you a lower price. If you try that new vendor, then the blockchain was just used for low cost customer acquisition. What's more, the third party motorcyclist enthusiast just built that app can also add a blockchain based gift card and loyalty program onto your blockchain, again that has no middleman or markup, so your users can earn points when they advise others how to fix their bikes, or stay at a hotel that caters to biking enthusiasts, or stop at cyclist clubs along the route you're planning for your summer road trip. And by the way, that app? Your blockchain is the now the appstore to sell the app through, right? So you're like Apple in this deal—it's all about creating the eco-system.

Is there more possible? Definitely yes, because the entire blockchain industry is right now figuring it out as we go. There is limitless potential for innovation here, but you need to move with some speed and spunk to grab your claim for 160 acres of the shiny new digital future. The greatest risk isn't from hackers, it's from competition. If you weren't first to market, then you'll have to compete against other blockchain startups. Again, it's a bit like DNS, in that the first person to register dirtbike.com got a major advantage over everyone else. So get moving!

Keeping it Simple

Let's consider the analogy of ERP for the design of blockchain applications. Studies has shown that the greatest pitfalls of ERP implementations have to do with trying to do too much, and ending up with a user interface that was difficult for staff to adapt to. These would lead to missing deadlines and exploding budgets, and inferior user interface designs that never got traction. The application of Agile process has been shown to alleviate the root causes for these problems. We can re-use these processes in the design of blockchain applications. The most important thing is to communicate clearly.

The second most important thing is to practice simplicity. The companies that insisted on overly complex and unnecessary amendments to the core platform usually paid the heaviest price. Vendors bidding for bespoke ERP projects were happy to promise the moon to nail that deal. This usually resulted in everyone shooting themselves in the foot. So, for blockchain applications, as much as everyone wants to promise the moon, it makes sense to keep implementations as simple and standardized as possible, focusing on the most valuable customizations.

The place where you will be tempted to add complex features are smart contract provisions. At the current time, it's probably smarter to keep contracts dumber... and focus on automating only those tasks that eliminate time-consuming human effort. Also, look for situations where a factual condition can be objectively ascertained, through programmatic reference to a database or a sensor.

Sophisticated commercial agreements, including matters that require subjective human judgment, are best left in human hands. A better term might be: "smart contractual provisions," meaning that the bulk of the contract still resides in the paperwork and a well-established legal framework, because existing legal frameworks likely already provide a reasonably robust basis for enforcement. Also, it would be wise to include provisions and code up front that deal with judicial enforcement and arbitration, to make it less expensive to override erroneous smart contractual provisions, if required.

Finally, it should be kept in mind that decentralized applications will likely lead to progressive decentralization at societal, legal, governance, and business levels. So when extrapolating your application usage into the future, think about how it will give increasing power to the edges of vibrant and growing economic networks.

Exercises for Chapter 4: Blockchains

1) Blockchains should significantly reduce the cost of multi-party transactions, how will it do so in your market of interest?

2) Blockchains require a standardized data format to accelerate the adoption; how would you structure the data for your market of interest?

3) Consider wire transfers... they now cost about $30, but become essentially free and instantaneous. Think of it as Skype for money. What's the Skype of your industry?

4) The web was really just one more way to stay in touch with customers, whereas blockchains are something new: they are ways to innovate faster with business models. How will you engage in business model warfare?

5) The iOS App Store is an innovation accelerator, which allows a $50,000 game to make $50 million dollars… think of blockchains as the precursors of a new kind of appstore, for distributed social and business applications. How would you design that appstore? What would be the top five best sellers?

_____

_____

_____

_____

_____

_____

_____

6) People who joined eBay sooner amassed more reputation than competitors. If you're first to the blockchain in your business, how would you amass reputation faster than your competitors?

_____

_____

_____

_____

_____

_____

_____

_____

_____

7) People who joined eBay sooner learned faster, how to be more effective than competitors. If you're first to the blockchain in your business, how would you learn faster than your competitors?

8) In the early days of the web, people who figured out why certain website designs were more effective than others got more visitors and promoted their small businesses better. What are the design principles that will give you an unfair advantage?

CHAPTER 5:
STEP 1: UNDERSTAND THE OPPORTUNITY

"I want to understand the world from your point of view. I want to know what you know in the way you know it." —James P. Spradley

HAVE YOU EVER NOTICED THAT SOME products, even when they have brilliant launches and huge marketing budgets, simply fizzle out in the marketplace? Market research and focus group tests indicated that they would be a hit, and bloggers raved about them and provided tons of favorable press. Retailers made big bets on inventory, but when these products finally hit the shelves... they totally fell flat.

What happened?

The most common root problem is that the developers of these products and services simply didn't gain a sufficiently deep and illuminating understanding of the people who they thought would actually use the product.

A primary means of accessing those deep insights is ethnographic research, which is also now being called "design thinking" or "design research." Just as marketers need solid market data and validated insights to guide their decisions about product positioning, revenue potential, and target markets, product designers need deep insights to guide their decisions about how a product or service is designed, used, experienced, and most importantly... its meaning to the user.

In summary, what's required are:

1. A deep understanding of the tacit needs, or hidden needs, of users.

2. An unbiased understanding of technical constraints and constrictions, and concealed opportunities embedded in whatever technology is going to be applied.

3. Clear and evocative user models that often take the form of user personas and cognitive workload maps; these are used during the initial design phases to model anticipated behaviors and responses.

4. Clear business goals. And since as the innovation process proceeds the goals are often going to change, it's necessary to keep track of the changes and make them explicit so as to avoid "scope creep" and misaligned expectations. These goals also define the targets toward which the scrum team is working, so clear goals are essential to enable the team to make the right day to day decisions, that is, to "self-optimize."

In summary, this initial phase of an Agile Design Sprint, which consists of two primary activities: domain research through stakeholder interviews, and inquisitive observation of users.

The scope of ethnographic research required depends entirely on the complexity of the product or vision. Effective ethnographic research can usually be gathered in a relatively short amount of time, but there is no set number of user interviews that are needed.

As noted above, as few as five to ten solid interviews may be sufficient, but note also that you can rarely schedule them immediately upon the start of the project. Instead, it takes time to identify who should be interviewed, and then find the actual people who fit that profile and who are willing to sit down with you for the three to five hours that are typically required. So while the interviews themselves don't require a lot of time, setting them up often takes a few weeks.

However, if the innovation under consideration is a complex system, consisting of multiple interfaces and user types, it may require twenty or thirty interviews to gather all of the relevant perspectives.

Domain research

Domain research activities focus on the past, the present, and the future. The design team should perform competitive research to identify past products, both those that succeeded and those that failed, to discover what you can learn from them.

Also conduct research on existing products and emerging products to understand what the market's needs and expectations are today.

For projects involving complex or technical products such as medical devices, it's probably essential to have one or more domain experts on the design sprint team.

Finally, don't skip or skimp on this initial research. Learning the basics of the product domain before conducting user interviews is invaluable because it will teach you the terminology and vocabulary used in the industry or consumer space; if you go into the interviews without that knowledge, you will likely alienate users and skew the data. Your grasp of the common terminology and practices not only builds credibility, it also streamlines and accelerates communication.

Internal Stakeholder Interviews

Of course the innovation you're working on will fit in some way with the existing corporate vision of the future, but it would be a mistake to assume that all of the members of your scrum team understand the totality of the corporate vision. We have often found that the vision which is so clear for senior managers is anything but clear for many others in the same organization. Sometimes a product vision has been completely mutilated to suit the unspoken agendas of middle management, while others weren't well articulated to begin with. Uncovering all of this up front can save a lot of anguish in the latter stages of the project.

If, for example, your company doesn't already have a very clear idea of what it wants to build and sell, you will never be able to design a product that meets expectations, much less exceeds them. The key, again, is to embrace multiple perspectives, and the best method may be conducting multiple interviews with internal stakeholders to identify what is and is not understood and shared throughout the organization. Knowing what the gaps are when you start will provide tremendous advantages and perhaps useful leverage as you go forward.

Observational Field Work

Product and service innovators certainly shouldn't ignore their intuitions about ideas that may become breakthrough products or services. At the same time, applying your powers of perception will expand your awareness and your creativity, and help you avoid creating designs based primarily on what you yourself know and like but with less attention and awareness of what your intended users will know and like in the future. Without expanding your awareness and informing your intuition about what other people want and need, your end product may not meet the needs of the people who you intend to buy it.

Ethnographic observation and interviews are thus central elements in design thinking and design research. The purpose is to study people's behavior in everyday contexts, rather than under controlled conditions such as a conference room in a focus group testing center, where the artificial nature of the setting inevitably distorts the information and muddies the interactions. To gain insight in a real world setting we often recommend conducting an "expedition" for the design sprint team during which they will visit real users in their real settings to observe what they do, and engage in dialog about what works and doesn't work so well.

Instead of formal questionnaires or a rigid set of interview questions, these techniques focus on informal conversation and observing the subjects in their natural habitat. This helps the team to uncover the true attitudes and behaviors of users, which will inevitably inform the innovation process.

Hence, the goal is not to create an extensive research report; you don't need to do what an anthropologist or social science researcher would do. Rather, the purpose is to gain an understanding of the users at a deeper level, to be able to step into their shoes during the design process and better anticipate features and functions that will delight them, as well as those that may dismay or confuse them.

Appreciation is central to ethnographic research – you appreciate their time and what they do. You appreciate the wisdom in their words by demonstrating genuine curiosity about not only what they do... but who they are. Hence, this form of interaction is sometimes referred to as "appreciative inquiry."

In addition to appreciation, the other secret ingredient in ethnographic design research is mindfulness. Mindfulness is the state of awareness that is characterized by a relaxed sense of volition combined with a gentle and sustained consistency of focus. By engaging in the ethnographic dialog in a mindful state, your attention is simultaneously focused both outward toward the subject, in full appreciation of their words and feelings, and inward with regard to your own emotions. Through heightened sensitivity you enhance your ability to feel your own emotions while allowing ideas to emerge, while still being fully present with the subject.

Successful innovations almost always evoke a positive emotional response, so perceiving and distinguishing the rich complexity of emotional experiences is a key component of design ethnography. This is vital for understanding tacit and unarticulated design needs, where emotions serve as markers for design opportunities. While engaging in ethnographic research your state of awareness is contemplative and cogitative, appreciative and discerning, receptive and creative.

Facilitation Techniques

This table lists some of the key issues to explore, research, discuss and gain insights through.

#	SUBJECT	ISSUES TO DISCUSS IN PHASE I
1	Define the problem	Create a crystal clear problem statement. Please contribute your thoughts about the problem we're trying to solve. The goal is to articulate the business goals clearly, which may affect features and product strategies downstream.
2	Painstorming	The key to a winning design is to focus on the customer pain points. For this, we must do some painstorming. PAIN = Persona + Activity + Insights + Needsmapping
3	Personas	It's essential to define who the users are. One way to do this is by creating "user personas." A user persona is a representation of the goals and behavior of a hypothetical group of users, which helps us focus on a manageable cast of characters instead of hundreds or even thousands of individuals.
4	Ethnography	Perform ethnographic design research to not only define how the product is designed, used, experienced, and most importantly… to find the meaning of the product to the user.
5	Stakeholder interview notes	Just as an idea needs multi-visioning, an organization's vision and strategy must be understood through a variety of perspectives. So let's interview the stakeholders and collect their perspectives here.
6	Competitive landscape	Discuss and review the competitive landscape. This is a good place to include photos and profiles of existing products to emulate.
7	Insights, blindspots, vision quest	Collect and itemize the insights and takeaways in this thread for easy access.
8	Success metrics	Identify the right success metrics to consider for this ideascrum.

TABLE 2: ISSUES FOR PHASE I UNDERSTANDING

Overcoming Resistance

You may discover, however, that your intent to engage in ethnographic design research is not received enthusiastically by your CFO or CEO—someone in a position of reviewing or approving your budget. In this case, you might explain that "an ounce of design research up front will save us a pound of pivot down stream."

A further indicator that design research will be exceptionally fruitful is when that executive tells you, "Why do you need to do this research? Just ask me! I know what our customers want! I've spent years in this business!" In response, you might point out that views and expectations are changing, and technology is changing, and its worthwhile to make sure that our understanding of current and future needs is up to date. If they say, "It feels like we're just re-inventing the wheel," you can respond, "Insufficient design research is the primary reason people re-invent the wheel, doing ethnography, design thinking and design sprints is exactly how companies like Apple and Google stay ahead of everyone else."

Final Tips

A few more tips for those who are facilitating the Understanding Phase:

• Each member of the team should participate in a few interviews so that everyone has direct experience of these interactions. Thirty to sixty minutes may be plenty of time, although much longer interviews may also be helpful. It makes sense to target about 10 interviews, which should provide abundant material to come up with the initial findings to inform an initial sprint.

• After the first batch of interviews is completed, get together and discuss the insights. As I noted above, the second half of the understanding phase is bringing the team together for an analysis of what's been found. During this analysis section, each person presents his or her research findings, and through team discussion we seek a common understanding of the research priorities of the problem statements.

• It may be productive to arrange a second day of interviews to validate certain findings or to try different approaches. You will also further iterate your research in the next sprint after developing prototype.

• To envision breakthrough products and services, it will be necessary to change the way we see before we change the way we think. Have team cross assess their findings to see if sufficiently bold ideas are emerging.

• The key to innovation success and sustained organizational profitability lies in understanding the unarticulated needs of customers, and then meeting them by anticipating their future or hidden requirements and ensuring they reach greater and deeper satisfaction than they could with a competitor's product. Hence, it's a good idea to cross assess research findings to see if unarticulated needs are being discovered.

• Invent new kinds of maps to help you understand the results of your research. These could be cognitive workload maps, emotion maps, process flow diagrams, or an eco-system chart. Who are the actors? What are the axes? Can you do it in 3D?

• Map stakeholders using analogies. Are they more like Game of Thrones, or Star Trek? Are their needs more consistent with Harry Potter, or The Office?

• Use the "How Might We" method to spark creativity. Write ideas on Post-it notes and cluster them to look for patterns or common causes.

• Set time limits on these elements of brainstorming and creative thinking, also known as timeboxing, which drives progress.

• If you're doing a design sprint with a group in person, find a dedicated space for the entire process, along with plenty of white boards, post it notes, multi-vision perspectives, etc.

• If you're engaged in a compressed, single day Understand phase then it's normal to do a few days of work to prep, as you'll need to collect and review the existing research, prepare a competitive landscape, list assumptions and potential blindspots, and schedule candidates for user interviews.

Exercise for Phase I: Understand

1) In your industry, identify a recent unexpected success. Why was it a success? Why was it unexpected? How could that success be replicated in a blockchain play?

_____

_____

_____

_____

_____

_____

_____

2) In your industry, identify a recent unexpected failure. Why was it a failure? Why was it unexpected? What can we learn about it to avoid replicating it?

_____

_____

_____

_____

_____

_____

_____

_____

3) Identify five ways that the blockchain revolution could change your industry.

1. _____

2. _____

3. _____

4. _____

5. _____

4) What are the various users' primary pain points? And how could they be addressed using a blockchain solution?

_____

_____

_____

_____

_____

_____

_____

_____

_____

5) Come up with ideas for...

Blockchain + VR = ?

Blockchain + big data = ?

Blockchain + machine learning = ?

Blockchain + healthcare = ?

Blockchain + cloud computing = ?

Blockchain + VR = ?

6) Consider the following thought provoking blockchain pilots:

Tackling human trafficking
One fifth of the world's population – an estimated 1.5 billion people – do not have an official document to prove their identity. Most of them live in Asia and Africa and a "disproportionate number" are women and children, the World Bank says. Without legal identification, these people are "invisible" to society, which makes them vulnerable to trafficking, prostitution and exploitation. Microsoft has announced it is working with partners on a secure identity system that uses blockchain to independently verify people's identities.

Tracking blood diamonds
The Kimberley Process, an international body launched in 2003 to clean up the trade in conflict-zone diamonds, is exploring how blockchains could help trace the provenance of diamonds. One start-up, Everledger, is already using blockchains to digitally certify diamond ownership. CEO and founder Leanne Kemp believes the technology could also be applied to other problems such as ivory poaching. "The question of authenticity is key because, for instance, counterfeit goods are funding terrorist activities," she explained in an interview with Wired Magazine. "We can apply this technology to solve very big problems: ivory poaching, blood diamonds, all these big 'blood problems' that are helping cartels, terrorists and criminals." The fashion industry is also experimenting with blockchains as a method of tackling counterfeiting.
Everledger is a company which creates permanent ledger of diamond certification and the transaction history of the diamond using blockchain. The characteristics which uniquely identify the diamond such as height, width, weight, depth, color etc are hashed and registered in the ledger. The verification of diamonds can be done by insurance companies, law enforcement agencies, owners and claimants. Everledger provides a simple to use web service API for looking at a diamond, for creating and working with claims by insurance companies, and for filing police reports on stolen diamonds.

Shaking up the music industry
In the music industry, the blockchain is being touted as a way to level the playing field for artists by allowing them to sell directly to fans and to solve licensing issues. Grammy-winning singer-songwriter Imogen Heap released her song Tiny Human using a blockchain platform. Users paid for licences to download, stream and remix the song, and each payment was automatically split between all the people involved. Heap has now launched her own blockchain project, Mycelia.

Registering land
Sweden is experimenting with putting its land registry system on the blockchain. The plan is to use the technology to make the details of real estate transactions visible to all parties – banks, brokers, government officials, buyers and sellers. For developing countries, building immutable title systems on blockchains could be a means of stamping out fraud and encouraging people to record unregistered land. It might also help banks to lend against land. In Honduras, one of the poorest countries in Latin America, US blockchain company Factom was reportedly in talks with the government in 2015 to create a decentralized database of land titles. Meanwhile, Bitland is looking at the feasibility of putting titles on blockchain in Ghana, where an estimated 78% of land is unregistered.

Voting

Elections require authentication of voters' identity, secure record keeping to track votes, and trusted tallies to determine the winner. Blockchains can serve as the medium for casting, tracking and counting votes so that there is never a question of voter-fraud, lost records, or fowl-play. By casting votes as transactions within the blockchain, voters can agree on the final count because they can count the votes themselves. And because of the blockchain audit trail, they can verify that no votes were changed or removed, nor illegitimate votes added. Follow My Vote is an example of one company developing an end-to-end verifiable online voting system.

Car Leasing

Visa and DocuSign unveiled a partnership late last year that used blockchain to build a proof-of-concept for streamlining car leasing, and making it into a "click, sign, and drive" process. The prospective customer chooses the car they want to lease and the transaction is entered on the blockchain's public ledger; then, from the driver's seat, the customer signs a lease agreement and an insurance policy, and the blockchain is updated with that information as well. It's not a stretch to imagine that a process of this type might be developed for car sales and car registration as well.

IoT

IBM and Samsung have been working on a concept known as ADEPT, which uses blockchain-type technology to form the backbone of a decentralized network of IoT devices. With ADEPT, which stands for Autonomous Decentralized Peer-to-Peer Telemetry, a blockchain would serve as a public ledger for a massive amount of devices, which would no longer need a central hub to mediate communication between them, according to CoinDesk. Without a central control system to identify one another, the devices would be able to communicate with one another autonomously to manage software updates, bugs, or energy management. Others are also looking to build blockchain technology into an IoT platform. For example, Filament, a company that builds a decentralized network using the blockchain (among other things) for sensors to communicate with each other, raised a $5M Series A, with both Verizon Ventures' and Samsung Ventures' participation.

Predictions

The entire research, analysis, consulting, and forecasting industries could be shaken up by blockchain. The online crowd-funded platform Augur hopes to capitalize on decentralized prediction markets. The company says it will offer a service that looks like a normal betting exchange. The entire process will be decentralized, and will not only offer users a place to place bets on sports and stocks, but on other topics such as elections and natural disasters. The idea is to go beyond sports gambling and create a "predictions market."

Ride-sharing

Ride apps like Uber seem to be the opposite of decentralization — that is, one company acting as a dispatching hub and using its algorithms to control its fleet of drivers and what they charge. Israeli startup La'Zooz wants to be the "anti-Uber," according to Bloomberg. It makes its own proprietary digital currency — like bitcoin — which is recorded digitally using blockchain technology. Instead of using a centralized network to call cabs, people use La'Zooz by finding other people traveling similar routes and exchanging coins for the rides. These coins can then be used for future rides. Users earn (or "mine") these coins by letting the app track their locations.

Gift Cards

Blockchains can help retailers that offer gift cards and loyalty programs make those systems cheaper and more secure. With fewer middle-men needed to process the issuing of cards and sales transactions, the process of acquiring and using blockchain-reliant gift cards is more efficient and cost effective. Similarly, increased levels of fraud prevention enabled by the blockchain's unique verification capability also save costs and help prohibit illegitimate users from obtaining stolen accounts. Gyft, an online platform for buying, sending and redeeming gift cards that is owned by First Data, has partnered with blockchain infrastructure provider Chain (pictured above) to run gift cards for thousands of small businesses on the blockchain — the new program is called Gyft Block.

Wills

Wills are a specific kind of contract and this makes them well suited to a blockchain smart-contracts solution. Blockchain Technologies Corp's legal counsel, Eric Dixon, states that, "Most will-related litigation involves challenges to the genuineness of a will," and that while a blockchain would not completely remove these challenges, its distributed ledger system would make it easier to identify factual information and dismiss claims that are without merit. Linking documents related to a person's estate through a verifiable blockchain system would give executors access to a more trusted pool of data than current systems, where documents from disparate backgrounds need to be sorted to determine their veracity.

Do these give you any ideas for something even more thought provoking?

CHAPTER 6:
STEP II: DIVERGENT IDEATION

"Brainstorming.... when ideas f**k like rabbits." —Moses Ma

THE DIVERGENCE PHASE IS ALL ABOUT taking this deeper understanding that you have developed about the users, that list of pain points you collated and those insights you generated in Phase I... and coming up with some truly kick ass ideas for solutions. Since the purpose of divergence is to come up with an astonishingly high number of great ideas, it enables the team to get hands on experience with ideation and envisioning, thus facilitating everyone to come up with better ideas and to express those ideas more effectively and fluidly.

Creative ideation is a lot like playing a musical instrument. If you already know how to play, you can skip this chapter and just go ahead and jam, but if you're a beginner to brainstorming then it's useful to learn some structured techniques.

As I mentioned above, our recommended approach to structured brainstorming is multi-visioning. This is an iterative process through which brainstorming is channeled through a variety of themes in order to generate insights across a range of perspectives. By timeboxing, setting time limits for each perspective, teams tend to diverge more quickly and effectively, to filter out less promising ideas faster, and converge on the most promising directions that will most likely bear fruit.

Multi-visioning is based on a method of "conceptually rotating an idea," filling it out so it looks good from all angles and perspectives. One of the roots of the method is art school, where they teach aspiring artists that learning to draw is really about learning new ways to see. Rather than looking only at shapes, for example, consider negative space and lines of energy. Hence, when asked how he created the magnificent David, Michaelangelo reportedly replied simply, "I just removed everything that wasn't David." The same thing is true for innovation, for it too requires learning how to see and understand in a new way, much like sculpting in that it may be viewed from all angles. You have to apply different "perspectives" as you create. As you walk around a model as you sculpt, you move an idea around your mind, and your mind around an idea, to get it to look right from multiple perspectives.

Multi-visioning is based on the creative processes used by Leonardo da Vinci, Albert Einstein, and the physicist Richard Feynman. Da Vinci believed that to solve a problem you begin by learning how to restructure it in many different ways. He felt that the first way he looked at a problem was usually too biased, but with each "shift in his mind" his understanding would deepen and he would begin to understand the essence of the problem.

Einstein said that he found it necessary to formulate his problems in as many different ways as possible, using diagrams and visuals. Richard Feynman, most certainly the smartest person I ever met, felt the secret to his genius was his ability to disregard how past thinkers thought about problems, and instead to "invent new ways to think." He called it "generating different ways to look at the problem, until you find a way that moves the imagination."

And of course moving the imagination is exactly what we aspire to through innovation, moving the imagination of our design sprint team first, in order to move the imagination of users and customers next. Hence, multi-visioning is one ingredient in the secret sauce of the Agile design sprint, which evokes better, more out-of-the-box thinking.

In practice, though, how do you "rotate" an idea? Simply by asking the right questions that lead the group ideation down different conceptual pathways.

As I mentioned earlier, in the innovation world, you become a great innovator not by coming up with all the answers, but by learning how to ask the right questions. These questions, which we also call "ideation lenses" or "brainstorming perspectives," are used to stimulate and propel design sprints forward.

Consider asking questions like these:

"How does the customer see it?"

"How can we enlarge this idea, maybe turn it into a billion dollar business?" "How would Apple do this?"

"How can we open it up, maybe do open systems thinking here?" "What's the eco-system for this product?"

"What does the user really want to do here?"

The key is that the design sprint facilitator assesses a team's strengths and weaknesses, and creates a list of useful perspectives that acts as a kind of prescription to improve the quality of ideation and increase strategic alignment in the team.

The collective prescriptions can be used and re-used throughout the organization, so if your firm has a strategic imperative to "go mobile" or "use more open source," then you can propose sprints for those perspectives. If yours is a company that doesn't have the natural tendency to do enough customer insight work before barreling down the development path, the facilitator can propose detailed customer insight be the focal topic for the initial sprint.

Additional tips

• For in-person Agile Design Sprints (in a physical meeting room rather than virtual), keep the energy level up by shifting perspectives frequently. When the energy dips, switch to a new perspective; you can always return to a previous perspective if interest or ideation renews in that area.

• If the team is going to do this in person (face to face), do a few ideation warm up exercises beforehand. For example, have the team practice applauding the loudest for the craziest ideas to insure this behavior persists throughout the process.

• Use "multi-visioning" to conceptually "rotate" an idea to fill it out so it looks good from all angles and perspectives.

• Use multi-voting to quickly identify the ideas that the team sees most value in. Each team member is given a certain number of votes (represented by sticky dots), and they vote on the ideas they think most compelling for the end users. They may put all their dots on one idea, or spread them out, as desired. Next, the team sorts the more popular ideas and works its way down to less popular ones.

During the divergence phase the goal is to come up with a plethora of ideas. Some of them will be robust and others far less so, but even some of the half baked ideas can be fully rounded to completion through the process itself.

Starter Perspectives

This table lists a set of "starter perspectives" to consider when leading an ideation or brainstorming session.

#	SUBJECT	ISSUES TO DISCUSS IN PHASE II
1	Start by emptying your idea teacup	In this perspective, share your initial ideas and thoughts, release them to make space for the more creative ideas. It's like the zen master who overfills the student's teacup… you have to empty it to allow new thoughts to come in. So don't worry if they're not amazing ideas, or are too amazing to share so soon… it's all good. Just release your current thinking until you don't have anything else to say. Once your teacup is empty, we can begin.
2	Open thinking	How can we open it up, maybe do open systems thinking here?
3	Deepen our customer insight	Let's become the customers and think about it from their perspective. What does the user really want to do here?
4	Let's map it!	Let's create a map of the situation. Let's start with a SWOT analysis, and maybe we can do a force analysis, a mind map, or an emotion map?
5	Let's get visual	Let's get visual and create Crazy 9's doodles about this problem. It's simple: take a piece of paper and fold it into 9 parts. Set a timer for one minute. Each team member will sketch an idea in one minute's time, and do that eight more times in a row.
6	Expand the idea	How do we "billionify" a half-baked idea? Many ideas may seem like small ideas, but in reality, they could be seeds of billion-dollar ideas, if we only knew how to enlarge, deepen and modify them. Or maybe turn it into a global idea?
7	Let's de-constrain our thinking	What if money, time, people, supplies are not issues at all?
8	Let's hunt for blindspots	What is known and unknown about our project? Once we map this out, can we detect a blindspot, either in the customer or in our thinking?
9	Let's reframe the idea	How do we flip around, invert, or reverse this idea? Turning an idea inside out may sound crazy, but it can lead to some brilliant thinking.
10	What is the eco-system here?	What's the eco-system surrounding our customer and solution space?

TABLE 3: ISSUES FOR PHASE II CONVERGENCE

Exercises for Phase II: Diverge

Rapidly design replacement applications for web destination sites:

Blockchain to replace AirBNB looks like what?

Blockchain to replace Craigslist looks like what?

Blockchain to replace Yelp looks like what?

Blockchain to replace HuffingtonPost looks like what?

Blockchain to replace Quora looks like what?

Blockchain to replace Google looks like what?

Let's flip the system upside down, what do we get...

Let's get visual and map how your system works...

Let's hunt for blindspots...

What is the eco-system here? Draw it...

Who are the best partners for us to go after...

Let's get visual and design the dashboard for your blockchain. Sketch it!

How do we "billionify" this blockchain?

What are some other multi-visioning perspectives to consider?

Fill in the blanks

INDUSTRY	TYPE OF INNOVATION			
	Incremental Innovation	Breakthrough Or Product Technology	New Business Model	Blockchain?
Autos	Airbags	Minivan	Saturn	
Personal Computer	Bigger Hard Drives, Faster Processors, Bigger Memories	PC; GUI (Mac; Windows); Ipod	Dell; Itunes	
Financial Services	Zero Points Home Loans	ATM	Charles Schwab	
Food / Grocery	Organic Produce	Genetic Engineering	Whole Foods; Newman's Own	
Airline	Frequent Flyer Programs; E-Tickets	Online Reservations	Southwest Airlines	
Health Care	Digital Thermometers	MRI / Cat Scan	Hmo	
Media	Live Remote News	Blogs	Cnn	
Trucking & Transportation	Cross-Docking	Bar Codes; GPS	Fedex	

Sketch four blokchain ideas visually

INCREMENTAL INNOVATION

BREAKTHROUGH INNOVATION

BUSINESS MODEL INNOVATION

BLOCKCHAIN

Blockchain ideation bingo round! Capture the gist of your idea.

What would the customer service system for a blockchain look like?	What would a blockchain be like, if Google did it?
What would a blockchain be like, if your only goal was to help the world?	What would a blockchain be like, if Ritz Carlton ran it?
What would a blockchain be like, if Disney ran it?	What would a blockchain be like, if you had an unlimited budget?

What are the five most important ideation perspectives/lenses for your business?

1.

2.

3.

4.

5.

CHAPTER 7:
STEP III: CONVERGE TO A DISRUPTION MODEL

"If you're trying to disrupt the status quo and beat bigger competitors, you're not going to do it by playing their game."—Dharmesh Shah

I N THE CONVERGENCE PHASE, THE GOAL is to distill the outcomes of divergent ideation to discern the opportunities where the core value lies. This allows us to concentrate and narrow the design process to focus on the most viable solutions, and helps the team to figure out what needs to be built, tested and validated.

The intent is to find the "spine" of your idea's story, the central core of its innovation narrative. Multi-voting and clustering techniques help to identify which directions are most promising, and the key elements that will shape the narrative. We then expand on these themes by developing the business model sketchpad that integrates many of the elements that define a breakthrough business model, as shown below.

So how do we get there?

Many startups fail because they waste time, money, and manpower building an unwanted product, instead of one that customers actually will pay for. The key barrier is often a lack of proper "problem understanding" from the very start.

We start by defining what a business model is: it's simply the story that explains how the solution to a life or business problem is created, delivered to, and valued by a customer. And it's especially suited for describing innovative businesses in a way that investors and stakeholders can easily comprehend.

If you're doing an Agile Design Sprint in person, put the blank sketchpad on a wall chart, and start filling it in from the left side. (If you're doing the design sprint online, put the digital template in a shared workspace and follow the same procedure.)

The very first step is a focus on the problem space, and one of the easiest ways to understand the problem space is to do a "PAINstorming" exercise to provide structure for identifying customer pain points and to rate the pain level associated with that issue.

PAIN = Persona + Activity + Insights + Needsmapping

Most great product designers are intuitive masters of PAINstorming, as they know that learning how to understand the problem is the key to finding the best possible solutions. And the initial key to understanding the problem is listening better and asking the right questions, which is the central purpose of Understanding, the focus of Phase I.

And now that we've progressed and our third iteration sprint here is building the business model context around proposed solutions, we will use that understanding of the basis upon which to explore the various business model approaches that could meet the underlying needs, and/or the emerging or future needs as well.

Hence, what's needed now is a discussion through which to evaluate proposed or alternative solutions. We can readily do that by filling out the canvas as above, and then thinking critically about the results. How, specifically, do the results you're proposing to achieve compare with the way that the core problems are being solved today?

As a general guideline, you should be targeting at least an "order of magnitude" improvement in either the efficacy or cost as compared with the current approach or solution. Hence, does your proposal meet these criteria?

Is your proposed solution really 10x better or 10x cheaper?

Is your proposed solution unique?

How acute is the customer's pain?

What is really causing the pain? (i.e., what is the underlying or root cause of the problem?)

How much will customers pay to solve it?

The Foundational element is probably the most important factor for the spine of your story. Have you identified any limiting beliefs or behaviors, or blind spots which would enable a disruptive innovation.

Business Model Sketchpad

PAINstorming

What problems are you solving?
How acute is the pain?
How much will they pay to solve it?

Solution

Top three features of what you offer

Unique Value Proposition

What is it and why does it matter?
Is it really unique or better? If not yet, how can you make it so?
To figure this out, ask yourself what is the one thing you were put on this planet to do? What is your passion?

Unfair Advantage

Can you be copied?
How sustainable is your advantage?
Can you build a moat around your business?

Customers & Channels

Who is your target customer?
What is your path to the customer?
How can you reach 10x more leads?
Who can you partner with?

Foundational

Where are the blindspots?
What are the limiting beliefs?

First 5 Steps

What are your first five bold steps to make it happen?

Costs and Hurdles

What are the startup/launch, customer acquisition and distribution costs?
Who are the people and what are the resources you need to make it happen?
How can you get started right away to validate the model?

Revenue Streams

What is your revenue model? What is your pricing and margin strategy?
When can you start making money, and when can you be profitable?
What metrics do you need to focus on? What is your business "swing thought?"

Product/Vision

Marketing/Execution

FIGURE 2: BUSINESS MODEL SKETCHPAD

So let's delve into this now. The foundational box is the key to the entire startup model canvas, and deserves a thorough analysis and explanation. First, my definition of "foundational" isn't the usual meaning – in fact, the entire canvas serves as the foundation so it's possibly confusing to you. What I mean by the term is that we need to look at the underlying beliefs that you subconsciously hold when you design your product. These limiting beliefs form "blindspots" that obscure tacit needs and unarticulated pain points. The detection and understanding of these blindspots is the key to discovering breakthrough innovations.

These blindspots are usually hidden in plain sight, and you will probably say, "of course, it was staring me in the face all along" after you see it. Another saying we use in America is that the fish never sees the water. It requires heightened skills of observation and interviewing to learn how to see these subtle dislocations of meaning and ritualized behavior. I usually tell people that true innovation is when you can see what is broken, when everyone else thinks everything is running just fine.

Therefore, the reason I use the term foundational is because once a blindspot is detected, this new perspective or worldview tends to "shift the ground you're standing on" and makes you rethink everything. This process is also called "reframing" or "the big aha" by some innovation experts. A foundational shift is one that literally changes the foundation of your entire business model, and is how breakthrough innovation happens.

Next, define your Unique Value Proposition. This central component is the heart of a winning business model, so leaving this box blank or coming up with a weak answer is a good way to insure failure.

Ask yourself:

> *Is it really unique or better?*
> *If not yet, how can you make it so?*
> *Why does it matter?*

If you find it difficult to figure out your Unique Value Proposition, you'll find that working on the Foundational box - blindspots and limiting beliefs – will help you generate thinking that reveals your unique value and approach.

The Unfair Advantage articulates the competitive barriers to entry that make a business plan compelling. What is it about your approach that competitors could not easily copy or buy? It's important to consider this in advance, as once any startup achieves some level of initial success competitors and copycats will try to replicate the product or the service and its underlying business model, and hence your ability to defend your position will become critical. Some competitors will propose to offer more compelling technology, while others will outspend you on marketing. How do you deal with that? Can you build a moat around your business?

The Unique Value Proposition and the Unfair Advantage are sometimes difficult to define if you have yet to distill the essence of your innovation; it needs to be different, and that difference needs to matter to customers. And then you need to pack it into a few perfectly chosen words. Fortunately, you don't have to get it perfect right off the bat. Like everything on the canvas, you start with your best thoughts and then develop it from there in a process of iterative refinement. Your answers in any given box may help to clarify your thoughts in other boxes, so as you loop through the steps in the canvas the quality of your thoughts in each topic area will progressively improve.

Defining the customers and channels and the revenue models and the cost structures makes the thinking process tangible and specific. Who is your buyer, and how do you reach them? What will they pay, and what are your costs (and therefore your projected profits).

Can you describe your target customer?

What is your path to the customer?

Brainstorm ways to reach 10 times more customer leads? Or 100 times more. Who could you partner with to expand your reach into new segments and geographies? Who "owns" these customers now and would benefit from partnering with you to bring your solution into their customer base?

Modeling revenues will surely involve some guesswork, but even though these may be wild estimates it's nevertheless essential that you also begin to think about when you can you start making money, when you might reach break even, and when you can be profitable.

While you're thinking about these elements, consider what metrics you need to focus on. Metrics should be stated explicitly in the canvas. Distilling your thinking down to a small set of essential metrics, such as revenue flow, market penetration, or profitability, is key to focusing your team on the factors that will enable success.

Next, take a crack at cost structures. These will include customer acquisition and distribution costs. What's it going to cost to get it built and to market? What about the people and other resources you'll need to make it happen? Finally, think about what you'll need to get started right away to validate the model even without being fully funded.

The Business Model Sketchpad that you've just completed addresses many of the most critical issues and questions that are essential to your future success. It is also a tool to help you find the central organizing theme, the spine of your idea's story, the central core of its innovation narrative. The "why" should be somewhere in the sketchpad, perhaps obvious and right out front, perhaps discreetly hidden. Either way, it's essential for you to find it, and to converge your team's thoughts and energies around making it explicit and compelling. Doing so becomes a transformative event for your entire team and will provide alignment, synergy, and abundant motivation for the work to come.

Innovators and entrepreneurs must understand not only what their invention does at a functional level, they should also strive to understand *why it matters*. Hence, the through line for an innovation is not just the core feature set or the "minimal viable product"—it's the *why*. You must articulate the meaning of the product, as well as its overall vision, to the team, the company, and the user/customer, and most essentially how it connects with the user at an emotional level.

This links the user's objectives together into a thread, and pushes the underlying concept forward to the expression of its meaning: you must not just focus on the what and the how, you must start with the why. Thus, the throughline acts like a compass, guiding the direction in which the energy of the company will flow constructively.

This table lists some of the key issues to explore, research, discuss and gain insights through:

Facilitation tips for the Convergence Phase:

#	SUBJECT	ISSUES TO DISCUSS IN PHASE III
1	PAINstorming	What problems are you solving? How acute is the pain? How much will they pay to solve it?
2	Solution	Top three features of what you offer
3	Foundational	Where are the blind spots? What are the limiting beliefs?
4	Unique value proposition	What is it and why does it matter? Is it really unique or better? If not yet, how can you make it so? To figure this out, ask yourself what is the one thing you were put on this planet to do? What is your passion?
5	Unfair advantage	Can you be copied? How sustainable is your advantage? Can you build a moat around your business?
6	Customers & channels	Who is your target customer? What is your path to the customer? How can you reach 10x more leads? Who can you partner with?
7	Revenue streams	What is your revenue model? What is your pricing and margin strategy? When can you start making money and when can you be profitable? What metrics do you need to focus on? What is your business "swing thought?"
8	Costs and hurdles	What are the startup/launch, customer acquisition and distribution costs? Who are the people and what are the resources you need to make it happen? How can you get started right away to validate the model?
9	First 5 steps	What are your first five bold steps to get started?
10	Find the spine	So what is the throughline of our innovation story?

TABLE 4: ISSUES FOR PHASE III CONVERGENCE

- *For an in-person Agile Design Sprint, clustering means moving Post-it notes to gather similar themes into clumps, and to look from all directions for the spine hidden in those clumps. Multi-voting allows a group to vote with sticky dots on the themes that seem worthy of note. Give three voting dots to each participant, and let them vote any way they prefer.*

- *A good way to find the spine in your story is to design a 30 second TV commercial about your product. What do you say? What are the visuals? What brings the sizzle? Storyboard it.*

- *Roleplay the user in a skit with your team mates. Like an improv comedy exercise, ask people to contribute an inciting incident, like reading a blog or having it recommended by a friend, and then an ending line for the skit, like "I never thought I could get it so clean" or "so my wife/husband told me never to do it again."*

- *Instead of Crazy 8's, do Crazy 9's in a 3x3 matrix. What do the axes represent? How about increasing stickiness? Or increasing craziness of ideas?*

- *Return to the central question – is this really my passion? If not, how can I make it my true passion in life?*

- *Remember that most startups fail because they waste time, money, and manpower building unwanted or unneeded products instead of ones that customers actually will pay for. The key inhibitor of success is a lack of proper understanding from the very start, so keep going back and refining the PAINstorming findings to stay on track.*

- *Identify and resolve intra-, inter-, and extra-personal conflicts that your product causes or addresses.*

- *Look for ways to "dream bigger" with your solution. How could you magnify its benefits and its impacts by 10x?*

- *Can you further minimize your minimally viable product? Is it still too bloated?*

Exercises for Phase III: Converge

A good way to find the spine of your innovation story is to design a 30 second TV commercial about your blockchain. What's the script?

Sketch the storyboards for this commercial...

Exercises for Phase II: Converge

Identify and resolve intra-, inter-, and extra-personal conflicts that your blockchain causes.

Intrapersonal

Interpersonal

Extrapersonal

Return to the central question – is this really my passion? If not, how can I make it my true passion in life?

Sketch how it all fits together

FROM YOUR POINT OF VIEW

FROM YOUR CUSTOMER'S POINT OF VIEW

How can you "dream bigger" with your blockchain?

Can you further minimize your minimally viable product?

What is the Spine of your Blockchain Story?

CHAPTER 8:
STEP IV: PROTOTYPE THE MVP

"Actually showing the product was powerful, because people were, to put it mildly, skeptical of the team's reported progress. They just couldn't believe progress actually kept moving at a faster and faster rate."—Jeff Sutherland

AS I MENTIONED ABOVE, THE PROTOTYPING stage assumes that customers and investors are all from Missouri... the Show Me state. Hence, the purpose of a prototype is to be able to show all of your stakeholders – users, customers, partners, investors, and your friends – how and therefore why your innovation is superior.

And it's true that nothing is more compelling than a good working prototype, which appeases even the most wary and pragmatic stakeholder. Hence, the real value of prototyping lies not only in its persuasive value, but in the validation it provides for the underlying concept.

In this phase, then, the team fleshes out the design to a level necessary to validate the core design direction. You can think of prototyping as a way to ask progressively better questions, which is actually the path to optimizing a design. Hence, some aspects of the prototype, those corresponding to what you want validated or validated sooner, may need to be more detailed than the rest of the prototype. Elements or aspects that there is certainty about may need not be refined or expressed as thoroughly as those about which questions remain. This is what innovation experts mean by a *high fidelity* versus a *low fidelity* prototype. High fidelity looks like the final product. Low fidelity is cheaper and faster to produce. However, you'll find that most prototypes consist of a combination of high and low components, as needs dictate.

For a first iteration, especially in a version 1.0 design sprint with only a day to build a prototype, a conceptual mockup is quite normal. This is sometimes called a "Powerpoint prototype," although it usually makes more sense to dedicate a few days to develop a higher fidelity and truly interactive prototype using a tool like InVision. If it's a later iteration and you're driving toward an MVP, a week or two for this phase is common, especially if the prototype will be re-used in many settings.

As noted above, Agile exists because traditional approaches to the development of large and complex software systems have such a consistent record of failure, and the inventors of Agile realized that the fundamental flaw lay in conventional thinking about how the work process was organized. Hence, Agile is a redesign – and a brilliantly successful one – that recognizes a better way to get this type of work done. Prototyping is an essential element of this fundamental reform of how we might more productively approach creative work.

#	SUBJECT	ISSUES TO DISCUSS IN PHASE IV
1	Define the MVP	Clearly define and agree on the feature set of a minimally viable prototype.
2	User testing script	Create a user testing script based on the tasks that need to be tested and the questions that need to be answered.
3	Find a tool	Look around for a prototyping tool suitable for our needs: InVision, UXPin, PowerPoint, or simple HTML/CSS provide acceptable prototyping media.
4	Timeboxing	Figure out the acceptable time and cost constraints.
5	Goals	Define specific the learning goals for the prototype prior to beginning the prototyping effort, so you know precisely what you're intending to measure and learn.

TABLE 5: ISSUES FOR PHASE IV PROTOTYPING

Here are some additional factors to consider when you're ready to kick start the prototyping stage:

- *The level of fidelity of a prototype should fit a variety of needs, providing the information a prospective and engaged user needs to grasp the intended experiences and its value proposition, the information the team needs to feel confident in their design, and which management needs to approve the project for advancement.*

- *In some industries there are rapid prototyping tools that can be applied to accelerate the process.*

- *For design sprints that are held in person, face to face, you'll find that working together on the prototype can also accelerate the entire process.*

- *We recommend spending a few days to produce a "high fidelity" prototype rather than just a mockup, as this will enable you to learn much more in the following validation phase. Hence, if "Powerpoint prototypes" haven't been adequate the last few times, move to InVision, as high fidelity prototypes are geometrically more convincing.*

- *If you're designing software, it really pays to have a good UX designer on your team. If you're designing a product, have a human factors specialist (who may also be a mechanical engineer). And if you're designing a service, make sure to have someone who understands experience design.*

Exercises for Phase IV: Prototype

What is the Minimally Viable Product feature set for your blockchain?

What do you want to learn from the testing of the prototype? Who is your ideal tester?

What tools do you have to rapidly prototype it?

What level of fidelity would you like ideally and what can you afford?

CHAPTER 9:
STEP V: VALIDATE THE VISION

"Every age has its particular form of epic storytelling, that reflects its culture and captures our hopes and dreams for a better world. Today, it's the elevator pitch."—Moses Ma

THE VALIDATION PHASE IS A REALITY check. In some ways, then, this phase is the flip side of the exploratory field work you did in Phase I. There you were seeking to identify end user and customer needs through needsfinding, whereas now the intent is to validate that the solution will address that pain that was identified. Hence, it requires the same skill set of empathic inquiry.

The process calls for a series of interviews with users who are hands on with your prototype. Observe how they interact with yours and with competitive products, and then interview them to learn what they experienced in their own words, and how they feel about it. The entire interaction plus interviews could last one to two hours, and involve at most two observer/interviewers so that the user does not feel intimidated, and can be encouraged to relax and explore and share their own feelings through the interaction and subsequent dialog.

Experience suggests that for a first layer of validation you need four or five subjects. The number five was originally suggest by Nielsen, who retrospectively analyzed eighty-three of his own product studies. "He plotted how many problems were discovered after ten interviews, twenty interviews, and so on. The results were both consistent and surprising: 85% of the problems were observed after just five people."[1]

If the findings are consistent then your validation may be complete, but if the findings diverge from one person to another then you'll need to do additional work to understand why an experience that was positive for some was not positive for all.

Afterwards, you'll compile your notes about what you learned into stories and observations that document the flow of interactions and key learnings. Next it's time to create the pitch for your innovation. Perhaps you'll craft an elevator pitch, or write the first press release, or come up with the first tweet or Facebook post. You could also create a "business panorama," a visual story-telling mural that effectively articulates the essence of your innovation. Share this with others in your organization, and perhaps your investors or key stakeholders, and fine tune it until it immediately evokes a deep understanding and appreciation for the essence of the innovation.

Central to all of these elements will be a story, the single most effective way to inspire a person, whether that person is a team member, an investor, a customer, to feel enthusiasm for your work. Since you've already been working on the throughline and central narrative, you can use these to focus on your story and tell it well.

The universal human connection to storytelling has a definitive physiological basis. Paul Zak, Director of the Center for Neuroeconomics Studies at Claremont Graduate University, notes that our brains produce the stress hormone cortisol during the tense moments in a story, which allows us to focus, while a story's happy ending releases oxytocin, the feel-good chemical that promotes connection and empathy, and triggers the limbic system, our brain's reward center, to release dopamine, which makes us feel more hopeful and optimistic. (footnote)

In one of Zak's experiments, study participants watched an emotionally charged movie about a father and son, and then were asked to donate money to a stranger. Those with higher levels of oxytocin were much more likely to give money to someone they'd never met, because the sense of empathy and connection they felt was elevated.

Successful storytellers focus the listener's minds on a single important idea, and it usually takes no longer than 30 seconds to forge an emotional connection that can add the special sauce of success to your venture. When you learn how to tap into the trust-inducing power of storytelling, your business model or business plan will exude not only crystal clear logic, but emotional alignment as well. This is a "next generation of a business plan," which is about the data as well as a living document that acts as an interactive operating guide for the venture.

---

1   http://www.humanfactors.com/newsletters/how_many_test_participants.asp

How to build a Business Panorama

To define the Business Panorama we merged the Business Sketchpad concept with the Ackerman Scenogram (see Figure 3 below), developed by UCLA Screenwriting Professor Hal Ackerman. The result gives the canvas a "story spine," which links the story elements in a logical flow and delivers an emotionally compelling ending.

Ackerman's brilliant model, which has been used by many Oscar winning screenwriters, shows how to create a visual representation of the story spine. All of the film script's key elements are represented, including the opening dilemma, the exposition, unifying devices, act structure and major turning points. This unites every element in a story,

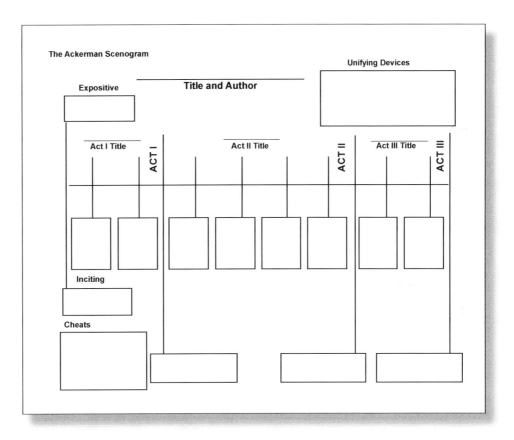

FIGURE 3: ACKERMAN SCENOGRAM

focuses it, gives meaning to events, and creates the forward momentum that advances the story to its conclusion.

Just as importantly, the spine tells us why things are important, and why viewers, listeners, or readers should invest their emotions in staying with the story to its conclusion. If any part is missing, then the spine is broken, a fully rounded story does not exist, and the writer can readily pinpoint where additional work is needed.

Adapting this model for innovation, it is often useful to think in terms of a three-act structure:

- *Act I: Describe the opportunity and all the assumptions necessary to make your innovation concept work, starting with an initial hook to ensure emotional lock-in.*
- *Act II: Describe the central hypotheses and techniques you will use to test and validate these hypotheses.*
- *Act III: Express the end state, the "happily ever after," in clear and realistic terms.*

The Business Panorama is a way to integrate the scientific, systematic, and rational processes that are required with both rational and meta-rational characteristics of observation, insight, intuition, communication, aesthetics, and empathy.

During an in-person Agile Design Sprint, a good first step is transfer the themes and concepts you developed in your business model sketchpad to Post-it notes, and kick-start discussion by reviewing those notes as you put them up on the business panorama wall chart. Explore and develop those ideas, and question their assumptions.

As you work to fully articulate the story you might realize that the underlying model still needs work. This is a natural part of the process and should not be a surprise. These things take time, and so when a playwright or screenwriter writes a first draft of the script, he or she often needs to hear the dialogue during a "table reading" with the actors to know if the ideas in his or her head really make sense when spoken aloud. Similarly as you develop the business model and start working on a panorama you should fully expect that you will tweak the model at a minimum, and even alter it in major ways.

In case you have doubts about the soundness of this, remember that the underlying business models of hugely successful companies from Google to Fedex to Facebook underwent massive change during the design, development, and startup process, and where they ended up turned out to be quite far from where they thought they were going. But in each case things didn't turn out so badly. It's now accepted as a given among Silicon Valley investors that the initial business model for a start-up has less than a 50% chance of being right from the beginning, and the smart entrepreneurs and investors are the ones who figure out sooner rather than later what the right business model really ought to be.

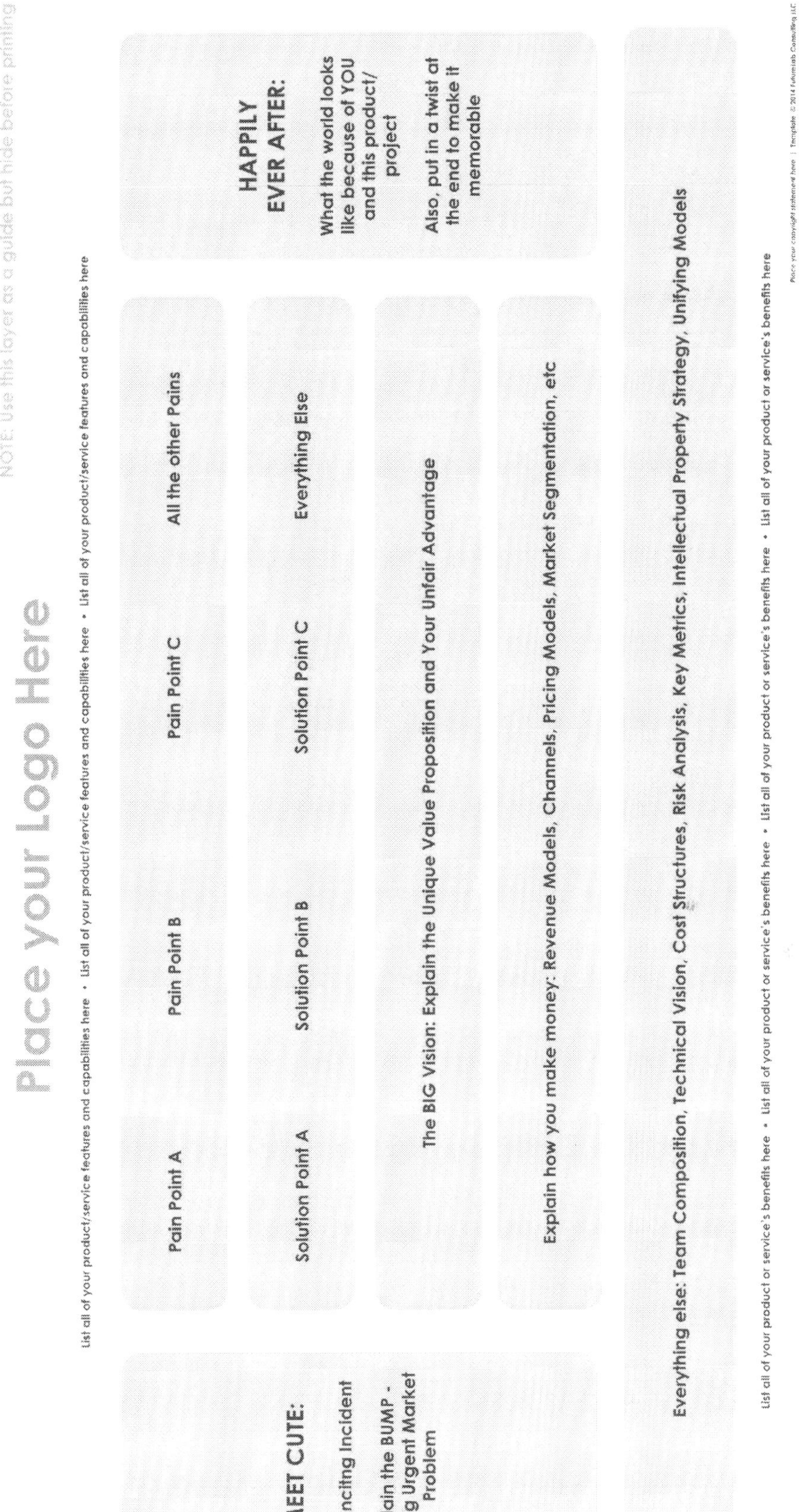
NOTE: Use this layer as a guide but hide before printing
Place your Logo Here
List all of your product/service features and capabilities here • List all of your product/service features and capabilities here • List all of your product/service features and capabilities here
MEET CUTE:
The Inciting Incident
Explain the BUMP - the Big Urgent Market Problem
Pain Point A
Pain Point B
Pain Point C
All the other Pains
Solution Point A
Solution Point B
Solution Point C
Everything Else
The BIG Vision: Explain the Unique Value Proposition and Your Unfair Advantage
Explain how you make money: Revenue Models, Channels, Pricing Models, Market Segmentation, etc
HAPPILY EVER AFTER:
What the world looks like because of YOU and this product/project
Also, put in a twist at the end to make it memorable
Everything else: Team Composition, Technical Vision, Cost Structures, Risk Analysis, Key Metrics, Intellectual Property Strategy, Unifying Models
List all of your product or service's benefits here • List all of your product or service's benefits here • List all of your product or service's benefits here • List all of your product or service's benefits here

FIGURE 4: BUSINESS PANORAMA

So where do you start? A good way to structure your approach is to consider the underlying structure of the story itself using this model: "A likable protagonist overcomes daunting odds by his/her own efforts to achieve a worthwhile goal." We can break this down into four elements: the character – your customer; the difficulties and pain points; the goal, the unarticulated need that is suddenly perceived; and the achievement of that goal – which occurs through your product or service.

To flesh this out, start at the top center of the Business Panorama template, addressing Pain Points and Customer Personas – the protagonists of your story. Describe the top 1-3 problems that you need to solve for your customer, and put them at the top, along with descriptions of your customers. We recommend leaving a space to the right for additional pain points that you have identified. Also, use visually pleasing and evocative images, and as many as possible. To fully grasp the personas, show their pain graphically.

Activities you can use, or questions you can ask, to stimulate discussion include these:

- *Brainstorm a large list of possible customers and customer types you envision using your product. This might uncover new pain points.*

- *Split broad customer segments into more narrowly defined ones. Even if you intend to build a mainstream product or a Facebook app, you need to start with a specific customer in mind. Identifying a customer persona will help unlock the unarticulated needs.*

- *Be honest, and consider if the pain is acute enough to generate a large enough total addressable market.*

- *Identify possible early adopters, and list the distinguishing characteristics of your prototypical early customer and your prototypical mainstream customer.*

- *Make sure the team identifies potential blind spots in perceiving pains or personas so that you can be sure to address and overcome them.*

Next, focus on the second strip from the top center, where you will record the solutions you are proposing that will address these pains. If you have a single product or service, then define the feature set. If it's a more extensive venture idea, the product will likely have several components.

Topics to stimulate discussion include:

- *Think about how these problems are solved today. Most problems already have existing solutions, so think about how your proposed solution is 10x better or 1/10 the cost. If it's not one of these, you have arrived at a very large red flag that may require some rethinking.*

- *Are there competitors, or is your solution truly unique?*

- *If you were one of the competitors, how would you expand your existing offerings to compete more effectively in the market?*

Next, focus on the third strip from the top center, the articulation of your Unique Value Proposition and your Unfair Advantage. This is a critical boxes on the panorama, and it's the one you absolutely have to get right. Distill the essence of your product or service into a single concise sentence that can fit into the headline of your landing page. This task will take some time, so be prepared to iterate a few times.

A tip from professional storytellers is The Rule of the Double Mumbo Jumbo. Veteran screenwriter Blake Synder explains that audiences, for some reason, will only accept one suspension of disbelief per story. So if you see aliens from outer space, that's fine, but if you throw in some vampires, that's double the mumbo jumbo... and your story's credibility is shot. Therefore, if you have two unique value propositions and unfair advantages, consider merging them with a unifying device to avoid discrediting your value proposition.

Some activities you can use and questions you can ask to stimulate discussion are:
- *How is this product or service truly disruptive?*
- *How do the components of the solution add together to form a unique offering?*
- *Does it have what's needed to overtake your biggest and nimblest competitor?*

Fourth, focus on how you expect to make money. This means you need to identify your revenue model, your proposed channels to market, and the flow of the money. Again, the structure of the story is more important than the numbers, so be clear about why it matters. This is the foundation for your positioning and branding, so it's the place to emphasize benefits and tap into emotion. This is your "high concept" pitch, your elevator pitch closing statement. Get it right.

A helpful hint is to consider the "business swing thought." A swing thought is an expression from golf, a technique that allows you to focus on just one aspect of your swing. Good swing thoughts cause a chain reaction of proper technique, so one thought influences the dynamics of your entire swing. Golf legend Arnold Palmer's top swing thought was "keep your head steady," a single thought that has transformed the games of countless beginning players. Apply the swing thought concept to an entrepreneurial venture to achieve a similarly transformative outcome. Here are some examples for you: Become cash flow positive soon. Maximize eyeballs. Available everywhere.

Finally, move to the "Happily Ever After" area to the right of the template. Many screen writers spend most of their time working on the first 30 pages of the script, and then the final ten pages are written in a panicked frenzy because the deadline for completion is imminent. But for the story's spine to be strong, the concluding section needs to be executed with the same amount of effort you put into figuring out your product. Hence, one of the rules of storytelling at Pixar is, "Come up with your ending before you figure out your middle. Seriously. Endings are hard, get yours working up front."

The need and solution boxes are the most important in a business canvas... but for the panorama it's the gigantic epic finish! If you figured out how to "open big," you must then figure out how to "close bigger!"

In narrative storytelling, this is also called The Third Act, and the entire craft of screenwriting is about setting up and delivering an emotionally satisfying ending to your audience. In your panorama presentation you need to do the same thing – provide a conclusion that is compelling, thought provoking, convincing, satisfying, surprising and unforgettable. It has to wrap up all the questions on multiple levels: intra-personal, inter-personal and extra-personal. Finally, describe that final grand shift in the worldview of the protagonist, resolving a critical issue in life, and leading to eternal happiness.

Here's a hint about it: nearly every Pixar movie ends as its protagonist achieves the goal that he or she was seeking ... only to realize that that's not what he or she truly needed. Often the protagonist lets go of what was desired in order to get what is needed at a much deeper and more profound level. Look at the blind spots revealed in the sketchpad to power the inner plot twist that deepens the spine of the story, and brings depth to the characterization.

As you take your time and work through all of this carefully, you may also find that it helps you to refine the initial assumptions and product concept... because you were probably focused on what the customer said they wanted, and not so much aware of what your customer actually needed.

Activities you can use and questions to ask to stimulate discussion include:
- *What does the world of the customer look like now that your product has transformed their lives?*
- *How did the happy ending resolve multiple goals?*
- *Was there an emotional, as well as intellectual, component to this ending?*
- *What is the deeper truth or the more profound insight that can be recognized and achieved?*

After this, we move back to the beginning, which we call "Meet Cute." This is the left side of the panorama, the scene in film in which the future romantic couple meets for the first time— in some memorable, adorable, entertaining, or amusing way. For example, in the romantic comedy, *The Holiday,* Kate Winslet's character and Jack Black's character "meet cute" in the driveway after she swaps her rural English home for one in Los Angeles.

The meet cute is often the hardest thing to write in a script, and it may be the hardest thing to figure out in your panorama as well. But if you get it right, no investor will ever forget you; look deeper into the blind spot to find a good Meet Cute setup.

The Meet Cute is also where you can "lay pipe" and set up a deeper payoff in your story. Normally when you present your idea you can expect that sales resistance is greatest toward the end of the presentation, so if you sneak in something—almost subliminally—at the beginning when their guard is down. This will help you with your close. However, be cautious about laying too much pipe. In movies, audiences will only stand for so much foreshadowing of it before it gets obvious and therefore tedious, and the same is true for business presentations. Do it cleverly, like framing the setup while relating an engaging situation.

The way to think about this is to see that the whole point of the beginning is to be somehow poetically resolved at the end. In terms of a business model presentation, the "meet cute" should ideally reveal the BUMP – the Big Urgent Market Problem - which is then reflected in your Unique Value Proposition and resolved in the Happily Ever After.

So after you have fun writing the Happily Ever After and the Meet Cute, go back over the pain points, the solution and your Unique Value Proposition, to ensure that everything fits nicely together.

Questions to stimulate discussion:

- *Why is this opener engaging? Who will it be engaging to?*
- *What is your Big Hairy Audacious Goal?*
- *What exactly are you laying pipe for? What is the big emotional payoff?*

Finally, across the bottom, place everything else of significance – team composition, technical vision, cost structures, risk analysis, key metrics, intellectual property strategy, customer testimonials, etc. Use as many visuals and icons here instead of words, as you can then refer to them if you are asked questions about your presentation.

Questions to stimulate discussion:

- *Which is most important to your organization, its mission, core values or vision?*
- *How will you be relevant five years from now? Why?*
- *Describe your corporate culture in three words.*

All of these elements are also presentable via Powerpoint slides, but in our experience Powerpoint decks are much over-used, and by doing something different such as presenting your model directly from the business panorama might get you some of the attention that you deserve.

Lastly, we've had success using the sequence as described here, but if your muse was gracious enough to gift you with the perfect opener or an amazing ending at the very beginning of your creative process, by all means accept that gift and go with it.

#	SUBJECT	ISSUES TO DISCUSS IN PHASE IV
1	Interview findings	Let's collate and note the findings from our prototype demos. What did we expect and validate? What didn't we expect? What blindspot did it reveal? What do we need to test for and validate next time?
2	Pain points	Copy over the top pain points from the Sketchpad and discuss.
3	Solution points	Copy over the top solution points from the Sketchpad and discuss.
4	The BIG Vision	Explain the Unique Value Proposition and Your Unfair Advantage
5	How you get there	Explain how you make money: Revenue Models, Channels, Pricing Models, Market Segmentation, etc
6	Happily ever after	What the world looks like because of YOU and this product/project. Also, put in a twist at the end to make it memorable.
7	"Meet cute"	The Inciting Incident. Explain the BUMP - the Big Urgent Market Problem.
8	Everything else	Put everything else here: Team Composition, Technical Vision, Cost Structures, Risk Analysis, Key Metrics, Intellectual Property Strategy, Unifying Models
9	The throughline	Let's get really clear on the spine of our story...
10	Remember	What are the key take aways for the next iteration?

TABLE 6: ISSUES FOR PHASE V VALIDATION

The next thing you should do is look for the "spine" of your innovation story. The story spine is a technique used in Hollywood to insure that a screenplay has zest, gusto... oomph! Otherwise, stories never seem to go anywhere. In short, the hero and the story are spineless. Innovations tend to work the same way; you need to help your innovation find its spine.

In the movie business, if your hero has no desire and does not feel any pain, then the story will have no purpose and it will be quite boring to watch. This happens when the writer hasn't thought things through thoroughly. Just writing and seeing where your muse takes you is a great method, but you must be careful when using this free form style, or your story will appear limp and lifeless. The exact same thing can be said of an innovation. Unless it is driven by desire, passion and pain – not yours, the customer's – it will perform limply at market. What you need to do is create a clear definition of what makes your product and business model "spectacular."

At Pixar, which was run by Steve Jobs, they use this formula for developing the spine of a story:

Once upon a time there was ___. Every day, ___. One day ___. Because of that, ___. Because of that, ___. Until finally ___.

These seven sentences will help the creative mind create a story and build it, scene by scene, to its climax and resolution. And it all begins with those familiar four words: *Once upon a time...*

Similarly, in the world of Agile project management, they use something called an Agile "user story" instead of a use case. These are short, simple descriptions of a feature told from the perspective of the person who desires the new capability, usually a user or customer of the system. They typically follow a simple template:

As a <type of user>, I want <some goal> so that <some outcome>.

For innovation, I've blended these formulae to help find the spine of the innovation story:

The <user persona > reports an issue <opportunity gap> with an unspoken pain of <pain point>, and I suddenly realized <blind spot> so the idea is to <describe the idea>. And because of this <impact to the world>.

Here is an example of this formula, used for a mobile app user story:

Alicia, a middle manager, reports an issue of task requests being forgotten when things get too busy. There is an unspoken fear of being unfairly blamed for projects falling behind schedule, exacerbated by people not reporting and dealing with blocks effectively. I suddenly realized that a lightweight form of Agile could be applied, so the idea is to make and track simple task promises effortlessly using a mobile app. Once installed, the entire group increases productivity significantly.

This isn't perfect, so if you can find some improvement to it, please let me know. But it should help you improve your blindspot detection capabilities. This is the key to powering innovation. Finally, you must always remember that true innovation is not about some technology – it is about creating a transformational change in the way people live, work and play.

And this is the model for creating a spine for a blockchain story:

THE SPINE	STRUCTURE	FUNCTION
The <type of user> reports a need <opportunity gap>	Beginning	The protagonist is established; the routine is described
that reveals an unspoken pain or fear <pain point>	The Event	An event breaks the routine, which allows the blindspot to be perceived
and we suddenly realized <blind spot>	Middle	A realization is achieved; this is the Aha!
so the idea is to <describe the idea>	The Climax	The protagonist embarks on the mission of invention
and because of this <impact to the world>.	End	The protagonist succeeds, and a new routine begins

TABLE 7: ISSUES FOR PHASE V VALIDATION

Oh, if you're stumped, ask five of your friends – from diverse backgrounds – to give you painfully honest feedback about what they think is holding you and your startup back from creating a really breakthrough product. Ask them not to care about what is possible or not possible; just think of a "moonshot" idea or feature that would take people's breath away. This process could be quite enlightening or maybe dismaying. But it'll move you out of your comfort zone.

Here's a handy reminder for how to detect blindspots and limiting beliefs, and to break through them:

FIGURE 5: BLINDSPOT DETECTION

A few tips for the Validation Phase:

- *By selecting the right test subjects, often "super users," you'll gain invaluable feedback regarding both the details and the broader context, which will enable you to truly understand what is working and not working.*
- *At the conclusion, document your findings by putting together a simple list of keyusability issues and learnings.*
- *It pays to retain a good UX designer to join your team.*
- *Reduce the panorama into a one or two minute elevator pitch.*
- *Map out the prototype flows, and look for your blindspots, assumptions, and overlooked or disregarded counter-indicators. If nothing else, it's better to know about them and be prepared to address them than to be surprised when potential investors or supporters surprise you.*
- *Be sure to ask for feedback that is effective by preparing your reviewers to provide clear and actionable suggestions.*
- *Are the test subjects sufficiently representative of your target user? Are they real users or just friends? Did you invite your mother or your spouse to attend because they would come, even if they're nothing like your target customer? If so, rethink the validation plan, as your data may not be as good as you want it to be.*

When you put some work into it, the panorama can make a really nice exhibit for your lobby, like this one we recently did for a technology project of ours. There's a ton of information here, and for anyone who's interested, a pretty good story too.

FIGURE 6: PANORAMA IN SITU

FIGURE 7: BUSINESS PANORAMA SAMPLE

Exercises for Phase V: Validate

What is the BUMP – the Big Urgent Market Problem?

What is your Unique Value Proposition, and how do you "lay pipe" for it?

What are the plot twists of your blockchain story?

What is the "spine" of your blockchain story?

How do you access emotion in relating your blockchain story?

Write your elevator pitch here:

CHAPTER 10:
STEP VI: THE INNOSPECTIVE

"Strive for continuous improvement, instead of perfection."—Kim Collins

THIS PHASE IS CALLED AN "INNOSPECTIVE," which is a modification of the Agile "retrospective." Retrospectives are used to continuously improve the Agile process by reflecting on the work that has been done, how it was implemented, and identifying how the process can be improved. The 12th agile principle states: At regular intervals, the team reflects on how to become more effective, then tunes and adjusts its behavior accordingly.

The whole team participates in the retrospective meeting, where they review how the sprint has been done, and consider what and how they want to modify their processes to improve the results for the next sprint. Retrospectives are thus an effective way to do short cycle improvement.

An innospective is much like a retrospective, with the addition of effort on finding innovations to significantly enhance the process, and on improving the process of finding innovations in future sprints and scrums. A typical retrospective follows a model of "Drop-Add-Keep-Improve," but we have found that the approach embodied in the photo below is also quite useful. The three segments are "worked/liked," "didn't work/ didn't like," and "insights/breakthroughs."

What worked and should be kept or refined, what didn't work and should be dropped or fixed... and what new ideas do we have that might totally disrupt the Agile Innovation world? Multi-visioning can also be applied to help come up with those new ideas, and you can also use each of the positives and negatives to inspire new perspectives.

In a software engineering setting it's common for the team to assess the results of their work in terms of product health, release health, technical debt, sprint cadence and the team's psychological well-being... which is also known as the "happiness metric."

This is also a good time to review the innovativeness and agility of the team, and to consider what investments we may need to make in our own basic capabilities in both technical domains as well as in our capacities as creative and innovative thinkers.

Some conversation starters:

#	SUBJECT	ISSUES TO DISCUSS IN PHASE V
1	Three words	On this thread, express yourself by sharing three words to describe your experience of this sprint.
2	Happy about…	What worked in this sprint and how can we improve it?
3	Need to improve…	What didn't work, and how can we fix it or lose it.
4	Ideas for improving this process	How can we improve the process we've developed? Who should we ask to join the team for the next sprint? What perspectives should we add?
5	Ideas for improving Agile Innovation	What ideas do we have for improving the core process of Agile Innovation to send to breakthrough@futurelabconsulting.com?

TABLE 8: INNOSPECTIVE ISSUES

FIGURE 8: ONE WAY TO DO IT

Facilitation tips for the Innospective Phase:

- *The One Word check-in is a simple activity that allows the participants to share their feelings before getting into the data and details for the meeting itself. It is a good opening for a meeting as it acknowledges feelings and get people to open up from the very beginning.*

- *Another option is to lead a Three Word Check In. The first word describes what you want everyone to think, the second word is what you really think, and the third word is where you'd like to go.*

- *It may be worthwhile to review input from previous innospectives and then seeing if the results achieved in this sprint were better than previously.*

- *Look for the root causes of aspects or elements of the process that didn't work. Use the "Five Times Why" exercise, a form of root cause analysis that gets to the deeper sources of problems, and helps you define actions that address them.*

- *As noted, use multi-visioning to generate better ideas for improving the process.*

- *Make sure to share a lot of appreciation. Thank everyone for participating, and respect that they did their best. Ask them what the organization could have provided which would enable them to do even better the next time.*

- *Never play the blame game. Make sure the retrospective is a safe place to express issues and concerns. There must never be a retaliation for thoughts and ideas shared here, or the value of all future innospectives will be nil. There must be trust throughout the scrum, or the process cannot succeed.*

- *Assist the introverts to share more fearlessly.*

- *Be sure to make changes after collecting the input during the innospective. The team will lose trust in and appreciation of the value of the process if no action items are implemented. Prioritize action items and create an innospective backlog.*

- *If there are lingering trust issues, a Strengths-Based Innospective that visualizes the strengths of your team members brings a solution-focused approach. Begin with a 360° appreciation circle in which each person writes down what they most admire about someone, writing it on a Post-it note, and giving it to them.*

- *Define and measure a Happiness metric that makes sense for your team.*

And now... congratulate your team! You've finished your first design sprint!

Exercises for Phase VI: Innospective

WHAT WENT WELL?

WHAT IDEAS DO THESE GENERATE?

WHAT NEEDED IMPROVEMENT?

WHAT IDEAS DO THESE GENERATE?

Do you have any ideas for improving design sprints in general?

Send them to us at breakthrough@futurelabconsulting.com!

CHAPTER 11: UNLOCK YOUR CORE CREATIVITY

"There is a fountain of youth: it is your mind, your talents, the creativity you bring to your life and the lives of people you love. When you learn to tap this source, you will truly have defeated age." – Sophia Loren

TO ACHIEVE THE HIGHEST LEVELS OF success, a specific set of creative skills is very helpful, including the abilities we've discussed in previous chapters such as the ability to see and listen deeply, to create and tell great stories, and to envision possible futures. But the most important is to unlock your own deep core creativity. In this chapter I'll give an overview of some of the key concepts and principles. To begin, consider that you already possess the most powerful computer in the galaxy – the human brain. This amazing tool was built to enable you to innovate, invent, and create, and it's every human being's birthright.

However, because we become who we are as the result of both nature and nurture, you may not have been taught to unleash the creativity which is latent in you. Like many others, you may experience inhibitors that get in the way. Let me explain by recounting a case history of innovation inhibited and released:

A couple of years ago, I ran an innovation assessment for a company that wasn't living up to its innovation potential. During the ethnographic interview process, they sent me only senior tech people, and I kept begging HR to send me some admins, customer service reps and QA engineers. It wasn't easy, because HR wanted a "good report" – they didn't realize that we needed to identify the core cultural inhibitors of innovation. Eventually, they did send me admins and secretaries, and one was notable – she didn't participate in the mandatory idea contest. When I asked her why, she said it was because she thought she wasn't smart enough. I asked what the prize was, and she said, "They were giving away an iPad." I asked if that was motivating to her, and she said, "No, I already have one." Then I said, "What do you think if I could talk your CEO into giving away something like... a free college education for your child?"

She stopped breathing. This, by the way, was a company in India where family comes first. She got this really serious look on her face and asked, "Is that possible?" I replied, "This is what I'm going to recommend, and explain that they aren't showing the level of commitment necessary to truly engage and motivate employees. Would this prize motivate you? Would you participate in the contest if there was a remote chance of something that could be so transformative?" She replied, "Not only would I participate, I would get my whole family to work with me to come up with the best idea ever so I could win!"

Step two. I then told her that she had five minutes to come up with the best idea of her life, and I'd tell the CEO her idea. She broke into a sweat, wondering if she were smart enough but then not caring if she wasn't, and I could see she was pushing herself to rise to a higher level of creativity, and in a couple of minutes, she came up with a really great idea. Then she asked meekly, "Is this a good idea?" I assured her that it was a terrific idea, and told her I'd relay this idea to the CEO with full attribution. Then several minutes later, when she was leaving, she said, "Wait, I have another idea!" She related an even better one, and before she left, she remarked, "Oh my god, I'm an innovator!"

The genie was uncorked.

Through many consulting engagements in which I've interviewed hundreds of people, I have finally begun to understand creativity and innovation culture. I've learned that great ideas can come from anywhere, but it requires for management to really understand leadership, and find the way to engage their employees fully, in order to motivate them to unlock their core creativity. So why are people inhibited in their creativity?

Here's a little test: Take a look at the image at the top of the next page. What do you see?

If you see the word FLOP, you are in the majority. But if you look a little longer, you'd realize that you can also see the word FLIP. The problem is that our brains are hardwired to see the negative first. Our brains are wired to notice danger first. This is because the brain first gauges the possibility of danger and failure using the limbic system, and only after the neo-cortex kicks in, to consider a possible opportunity. Innovators slowly learn to flip that around, and thus to operate more freely. It's a little bit like photojournalists who train themselves to run toward explosions and gunfire, instead of away from it like everyone else.

So how do you actually do that? Steve Jobs once said, "Let's go invent tomorrow rather than worrying about what happened yesterday." He wanted his team to stop worrying and kvetching about whether they could innovate, and get out there and actually innovate.

Another key to innovation is being alive to the entire spectrum and totality of life, and being open to its wonders and beauties. When you go to art school, you'll spend most of the first year not about learning how to draw, but learning how to see, and this developing deeper power of observation beyond the simple and material facts of everyday life. You'll learn about "negative space," the spaces between objects, and about composition and color. And gradually you'll learn to see into the significance of mundane things you observe, and they will not be mundane any more.

Developing your skills in innovation will take you on a similar journey, although instead of expanding your visual skills of observation you'll expand more broadly to amplify your overall awareness and consciousness.

The Three Shifts to Creativity

You can increase your own creativity by making three fundamental shifts in your patterns of awareness.

The first shift comes in learning how to expand the way you see. Just as in art school, you have to learn how to observe things at a deeper level. For artists, this means grasping the essence of the form, both the positive and the negative spaces of and around objects; for innovators, a critical skill is design ethnography, the practice of detecting tacit or unarticulated needs through observation.

The famous Apple *Think Different* ad campaign noted, "Here's to the ones who see things differently - they push the human race forward, and while some may see them as the crazy ones, we see genius, because the ones who are crazy enough to think that they can change the world, are the ones who do."

A useful definition of innovation is that it's really about seeing how things are actually broken when everyone else thinks they're just fine. Hence leading product development companies like Apple and BMW use design ethnography as a secret weapon to discover things about their customers that enable them to differentiate. Breakthroughs often come by shifting the way you observe customers, interview them, and then detect discrepancies between what they say and what they do. Applying these enhanced techniques for seeing and listening derived from anthropology yield insights that reveal disruptive product opportunities, pushing yourself into perspectives that are out of the box so you can think out of the box.

The second shift is learning how to expand the way you think. Albert Einstein quite famously said, "Problems cannot be solved by the same level of thinking that created them." You know that you need to think differently than you normally do to unlock creative insights in yourself and your team. You can do this by making multi-visioning second nature, which we described in Chapter 6 on divergent thinking.

The third shift is learning how to expand the way you believe in yourself. When your head is filled with limiting beliefs there's just no room to be creative. Hence, liberating yourself from these constraints may require some deep self-examination, but the time you invest in this will be well worthwhile.

By enabling these three shifts the native creativity with you and your team will be unleashed. Remember, though, your creativity needs to be exercised and refined on a daily basis; it's a skill, and like any skill from sports to art to music to writing, and skills typically require thousands of hours of training and practice to attain mastery. Ideation, the skill of creating ideas that solve critical problems, is no different. Ask yourself how many hours you and your team have invested in perfecting the skill of ideation.

The Neurophysiology of Innovation

So if you're inhibited in your inventiveness, how do you reverse that? How do you overcome your early life programming that created these attitudes that constrain your capacity for creativity? To do so, we must first understand the neurophysiology of creativity and innovativeness.

The act of creativity is a biological process. And like many other cognitive and biological activities, it involves the release of endorphins in the brain. Consider for example, the sexual reaction cycle, which has four general phases: the arousal phase, the plateau phase, the orgasm phase and the relaxation phase. It may surprise you to know that the innovation process follows the same structure.

For innovators, the arousal phase starts with that first inkling of an idea... a notion that teases the mind. The plateau phase consists of working through possible solutions in your mind, constructing a mental map of the solution in your mind. This is where you work it in your head over and over, in and out, back and forth... until you reach the Eureka! phase and start shouting because it feels good in your brain. Finally, there's the relaxation phase... that moment after conception that you realize that with your idea, world domination just might be possible.

This is more than just a humorous analogy. The brain works the way it works for a reason. Neuro-hormones require time and certain activation processes to function, replicating the stimulation and climax processes, followed by a relaxation phase that provides a refractory period before you can do it again.

This leads us, as both behavioral scientists and innovation consultants, to wonder if something like sex therapy could be applied to creativity and innovation. In other words, if your creative response has been sluggish or not as energetic as it was when you were younger, would it be possible to modify and re-purpose the treatment protocols of sex therapists... and adapt them to business innovation?

So let's jump in and give this idea a good think...

A good sex therapist doesn't get all technical up front, like starting off with, "Now here's a diagram of your clitoris" or jumping to the benefits of the coital alignment technique. They know that the right way to address sexual dysfunction is to first adjust the mindset. So that's where we must start as innovators, to advocate a mindset of creativity.

Next, a good sex therapist will talk about not taking it so seriously, and giving yourself permission to be more playful in the bedroom. Often, when a sex therapist asks a new client, "When was the last time you had fun during sex?" The typical response will usually be for the client to present an expression that says, "I didn't even realize that was an option." It's totally understandable to have some anxiety about the most important thing in your life, but the very first step is to lighten up. The same thing goes for brainstorming. Don't take things so seriously. Be more playful. Find the power of laughter.

When they get to the core of the issue, the sex therapist will likely explain that the secret to healthy sexual function is prioritizing pleasure. This is one of the simplest but most powerful lessons, because it takes the pressure off of performance. It is the core of Masters and Johnson's breakthrough work—known as Sensate Focus Technique— which helps couples rediscover pleasure without the pressure of performance, while learning enhanced communication skills.

And so, we call our approach to regaining expanded ideation capacity "sensate focused creativity retraining." The basic concept is that participants in a brainstorm should focus on the pleasure of ideation and creativity, rather than impressing the boss, worrying about the deadline and having huge expectation in terms of end goals. The point is that the act of inventing something is fundamentally pleasurable to the brain, just like sex. So the natural way is to "follow your bliss." If participants in a brainstorm, or partners in bed, are smiling and laughing and playful, it's a sign of success. These innovators achieve a state of peak performance, when ego dissipates into pure creativity and adrenaline.

Also, just as good communication is key in the therapeutic realm, this translates over to ideation and creativity as well. In a brainstorm, it's a shared dance of mutual support and admiration that works the best. When one participant, for example a less innovative CEO, starts barking that a certain contribution is dumb, it's just like one partner being rude and dismissive to the other in bed, blaming them for their own sexual inadequacy.

Any good brainstorm facilitator will tell you that the first sign of "this idea won't work" will constrict and throttle the flow of ideas. The best way to enhance group creativity is to suspend judgment—to first come up with lots of crazy ideas initially, and winnow them down in a later phase. But in the initial phase, there needs to be absolutely zero judgment and critical filtering and a 100% focus on encouraging divergent thinking. This means that for the facilitator, it's all about sensing the energy of the room, keeping that energy stimulated, and chasing that energy to a good conclusion. One exercise we practice in brainstorming workshops is wild approval and applause.

Also, directing focus and attention to the pleasure your brain feels during creativity can alleviate self-doubt. It's especially hard to feel worried about not feeling smart enough when you've just come up with the best idea of your life. Tuning into pleasure instantly helps you be more present in the moment. Neither sex nor ideation are fun when you're distracted by your self-doubts, whether they're about cellulite or your recently failed project.

Now here's the rub – the ability to feel pleasure is a skill, and like other skills, it requires daily practice. We tell our clients that human skill requires thousands of hours of practice to gain and refine a core skill. Learning how to enjoy the present moment, especially during the more mundane aspects of your daily routine, is most definitely a skill.

Beyond the Brainstorm

This view of ideation as a biological act helps us in other ways. For example, an effective sex therapist working with people suffering from intimacy anxiety, will need to teach new skills around initiation and rejection management. Unskilled initiation and rejection are toxic to intimate relationships, and similarly to innovation. In the sex therapy world, the typical pattern is that the partner with higher desire gets tired of being turned down and stops initiating. Pretty soon, both parties spiral downward into a sexless marriage, filled with covert hostility and complaints to friends.

The exact same thing can hamper an innovation team in a company. Rejection of new ideas, due to overly risk adverse management that is intolerant of failure, will stifle innovation. So will unskilled initiation, by people who don't understand the needs of management, and the requirement for strategic alignment of innovation with those greater goals of the organization.

Both are caused by an underlying inability to sense what the other is feeling. For innovators, it's important to listen to management's needs as carefully as you would to a romantic partner. Understanding their needs will lead to yes's. For management, it's important to listen harder to ideas from the rank and file, because the less you listen, the less they'll innovate in your behalf. Don't immediately turn your people down, even if "hell no" is your first inclination. See if you can find even the smallest part of yourself that would be open to the idea. Try to feel the pleasure in connecting with this person, even if you're under tremendous pressure to "produce results."

Sometimes sex therapists will meet with older couples who have stopped having sex entirely. Like, no sex for decades. The same could be said for older corporations, where innovation has died long ago and everyone is on auto-pilot for the paycheck, and dying to jump to a competitor if only they could land that job. At these companies, which rarely brainstorm in any meaningful way, "coming up with new ideas" is scheduled like sex for a couple that's lost the energy and excitement that brought them together in the first place. I've attended some in the past, and it's like that movie *Joe and the Volcano*... flickering florescent lights, a fatigued team, a facilitator demanding results as a way to stimulate ideation, patriarchal power structure... heck, even the food was lousy.

If you think about it, the job of an innovation consultant is a lot like that of a sex therapist helping a couple that has stopped having sex, and ruminating only on the negative situation, without the courage to make a change. These couples desperately want to find love again, but they just don't know how. Couples who tend toward silent rumination about what has gone wrong in their lives, reviewing the past selectively (emphasizing the negative aspects), turning every little setback into a catastrophe, dreaming up future disasters or engaging in self-blame—they tend to stay locked into a state of helplessness and depression.

In psychotherapy, research have shown that changing the underlying process, called 'reframing', can create a new frame of reference that makes change easier to achieve. What a sex therapist would tell the couple is to start slow, to find ways to warm up, to feel sexy, to sexify the brain, and focus on sensation instead of negative thoughts. They might suggest reading erotica or watching porn together, and talking about what turns them on. Or they might suggest going to a tantra workshop together.

This is equivalent to an innovation consultant who suggests producing an innovation contest, building an innovation library, setting up an innovation training, or trying a hackathon. You can't change the culture overnight, you have to start with baby steps.

But at the same time, it isn't enough just to do the small steps, you need to commit to a comprehensive program of change. And sometimes you need to do something more radical to reframe the thinking. Our goal is to "move the needle" as quickly as possible, so in our MindSpark! innovation workshops, we usually offer more dramatic techniques that include activities like firewalking and walking over broken glass, to change thinking and reframe what's possible. The increased level of adrenaline usually helps.

In both love and innovation, you have to make a commitment to keep it fresh, to make an effort to keep things novel, fun, exciting, and playful. There is always something new to learn and try, if you simply open your eyes and heart and mind. It is possible to keep the yum in the scrum, and the mint in the design sprint.

Formula for Creativity

There is a neurophysiological basis of creativity, and some terrific research is being done by John Kounios, a professor of psychology at Drexel University, that maps how creativity and insightful thinking begins in the brain, using EEG and fMRI to look at changes in the blood flow in the brain and showing where brain activity is happening. As a result, there are some very simple things you can do to provoke and support insights, out-of-the box thinking, and creativity.

There's a controversy in the brain science world about whether thinking changes gradually over time—what's called continuous processing—or if the brain snaps from one state to another state to another state more dramatically. The thinking at the time was that all thought was processed slowly, and that what people thought of as insight was just an emotional embellishment at the end of the slow thinking process that made it feel sudden. In his experiments, using anagrams to rearrange letters to find a word, they found that some people—instead of processing slowly—go from having no idea about the solution, to having the solution in one jump. This is the brain science view of insight – suddenly getting the solution. The slower process is called the analytical approach.

Kounios says, "Insight is like a cat. You can't order it to appear. You can't command it. But you can coax it. Creativity and insight flows from a particular brain state. And if you can put yourself in this brain state, you will be more likely to have these creative insights."

And from this, and a number of other studies, he found factors that helped improve creativity, from maintaining a more positive mood, to accessing more of the visual cortex, increased activity in the anterior cingulate—right in the middle of the head, taking a break to relax, to getting enough sleep to enhance "memory consolidation" that brings out hidden relationships and associative processing—the stuff of creativity and insight.

From this, we've developed a little formula for enhancing your personal creativity. It comes in a little mnemonic that spells out the word "creative."

Courage
Relax
Energy
Activate
Training
Inspiration
Visualize
Expand your thinking

Courage — Ditch your comfort zone. The comfort zone is creativity's nemesis. And getting out of it takes some courage. It's why we use fire and glass walks to help in this process of expansion, but you don't need to walk over broken glass. You can simply drive a new route to work, or take a vacation somewhere exciting, or do something you've never done before. Moving past your fear releases energy, and this is probably the most powerful creativity tip we can share with you.

Decades ago, brain research showed, using mice in a maze, that learning is enhanced when they injected norepinephron, a form of neural adrenaline. So a little stress that triggers adrenaline can actually increase brain function. Of course, too much stress and fear and the brain will shut down and enter fight or flight mode. But having a little skin in the game actually increases brain function and creativity. The best example of this was mission control coming up with 45 solutions to save the astronauts on Apollo 13. When the lithium hydroxide CO_2 scrubbers failed, they had to figure out a way to solve the problem in 24 hours.

Relaxation — Creativity uses a subtle voice, and the demands of the day will drown it out. Thus, sometimes your best ideas will come when you're not wracking your brain trying to come up with the next great idea. It could be while you're sleeping. It could be while your mind wanders in the shower that you get a great idea. So if your creativity is lacking, unplug. Relax. Be quiet and let your brain do its magic. In fact, researchers at the Australian National University found that subjects were able to solve problems about 10 percent faster by simply lying down than standing. Maybe it brings more blood to the brain, but more likely it's because you're relaxing.

By the way, the average person in America sits between 7 and 15 hours every day. It's terrible for your health and your mood, not so good for your creativity. Research at Stanford University has shown that going for a walk improves creative thinking. Priceline Group CEO Darren Huston, Facebook CEO Mark Zuckerberg, Twitter cofounder Jack Dorsey, LinkedIn CEO Jeff Weiner, and scores of other business leaders and entrepreneurs regularly have walking meetings. Creative thinkers have a habit of taking long walks to get their thoughts and blood going.

Finally, have you ever noticed that giving advice to a friend is easier than solving your own problems? This is because you are "psychologically distant" from your friend's problem, meaning that the issue is not occurring in the present and does not affect you. Therefore, you are able to think in a less concrete yet creative way. According to a study from Indiana University, increasing the psychological distance between you and a problem boosts your creativity. You may also gain new insights and clarity by thinking about a problem more abstractly. This is a form of mental relaxation.

Energy — Psychologist Mihaly Csikszentmihalyi coined the term "flow" to describe the way artists, athletes and musicians become so focused on their work that time seems to slip by. Virgin CEO Richard Branson once said, "In two hours [in a flow state], I can accomplish tremendous things . . . It's like there's no challenge I can't meet." However, it takes some training to achieve flow, which we teach in a workshop called Focus Lab, and it requires learning certain meditative techniques to develop a kind of energy that can be used for achieving focus and flow. We call it "zenenergy," which is sort of a directed energetic form of mindfulness, and it can be achieved through a committed daily practice of both physical and mental exercises.

You can also increase creativity by lessening emotional attachment to your project, a process called "psychological distancing." Have you ever shown your project to a friend and received a ton of useful feedback on things you've never noticed before? That's because you're psychologically too "close" to your own work, making you less able to come up with new creative insights, according to a study by Indiana University. It's good to lift above the work, in what mindfulness experts called the "witness state."

Finally, Americans are heavily sleep deprived, so it might help to take a short power nap, which boosts your brainpower. Both Thomas Edison and Salvador Dali— the father of surrealistic art – would take short naps to access the hypnogogic state between sleeping and wakefulness. Edison used a heavy ball bearing that he'd drop just as he fell asleep, to wake exactly at that boundary. Dali would put a tin plate on the floor and then sit by a chair beside it, holding a spoon over the plate. When he dozed off, the spoon would land on the plate and make a loud noise, waking him up to capture the images in his mind. This is known as the theta brainstate, which is considered to be a doorway to meaningful and creative mental activity.

Activate — By activate, we mean to activate your brain function. This could mean getting more sleep or drinking nootropic concoctions to give your mind a boost. Nootropics can be as simple as caffeine, or could mean "smart drugs" that include certain prescription medications, supplements and nutraceuticals, like modafinil and armodafinil. However, we really don't recommend it, especially amphetamines like

Adderall which are addictive and probably deplete certain neurohormones that cause withdrawal.

There's a natural way to increase those neurohormones. Do you remember the finding that before a flash of insight, there was more activity in the anterior cingulate, right in the middle of the head? That's the location of the pineal gland, which produces melatonin and more. According to Rick Strassman, Clinical Associate Professor at the University of New Mexico School of Medicine, has theorized that the human pineal gland is capable of producing the hallucinogen N,N-dimethyltryptamine (DMT) under certain circumstances. The pineal gland has been associated with the Hindu concept of the third eye chakra, which meditators focus on, hoping to activate it. In fact, some meditation schools run "dark room workshops," where you live and meditate in light sealed dark rooms, to promote the production of melatonin and DMT, which is said to repair sleep processes, and promote creativity.

Training — Creativity is like a muscle. It must be stretched, challenged, and occasionally pushed past its comfort zone. It's also a skill that requires training. The human brain requires roughly 5,000 hours of training and practice to master a skill, and creativity is no exception. You have to commit the time developing the skill. But it doesn't have to be painful! For example, taking an improve comedy workshop is a great way to teach yourself how to stretch your imagination on demand. Another thing you can do is create a "creativity ritual" that can become part of your daily routine. Thomas Edison had an idea quota, where he trained his brain to invent better, faster and deeper.

Also, take time to improve your observational skills. Stanford professor Tina Seelig says that "the more attention you pay to things, the more opportunities you see." Train yourself to be more observant, and you'll be more creative. You can also talk to mentors, or experts, and reside in a state of appreciative inquiry.

Inspire — To access your muse, you must focus on what you love. Love and creativity are intertwined. In a letter to his son, Albert Einstein addressed his son's interest in playing the piano, "The way to learn the most, is when you are doing something with such enjoyment that you don't notice that the time passes. I am sometimes so wrapped up in my work that I forget about the noon meal." So do something that truly pleases you, in order to lose yourself in the creative process: do something that pleases you.

Another way to get inspired is to hang out with creative people. A study found that "creative work is sensitive to the social context of the creator." Spending time with creative people—who enjoy their creativity as a model for you—and people who urge you to be more creative, are great ways to boost your creative spirit.

Visual — When it comes to visual thinking, many people immediately get hung up on the idea that visual thinking is drawing – it's not. Visual thinking is about bypassing the critical conscious mind to access the subconscious, which allows for improved creativity and problem solving, over using language or words alone. This is because visual thinking is the natural language of the subconscious mind. For example, if you're taking notes from a speech, when you think textually, you'll simply copy down word for word what the speaker says. But if you're thinking visually, you are interpreting their words and trying to find the meaning of what is being said. Visual thinking methodologies have been proven to increase understanding, improve retention and effectively communicate information.

It's a body of methodologies that uses diagrams to represent ideas, concepts, process flows and relationships. You can call this process idea mapping, that makes it easier to co-create ideas, both with others, but also within different parts of yourself, like when your subconscious emerges while you doodle. Thus, we use visual thinking to engage both the logical and creative sides of our brains, to increase clarity, to reveal connections, to see the "big picture" — stuff that might be missed in a strictly linear form. So try using a sketchbook to sketch your ideas. Try taking a graphic recording workshop. Try drawing your ideas out.

Expand your thinking — Researchers have noted that creative people tend to re-conceptualize problems more often before starting a creative task. As Einstein once said "If I had an hour to solve a problem I'd spend 55 minutes thinking about the problem and five minutes thinking about solutions." So instead of looking at the end goal of a creative project, it's better to re-visualize the problem from other, more meaningful angles before starting. We call this process "multi-visualizing," but there are other approaches. You could use the Six Thinking Hats technique. In this exercise, you approach a subject as well as your judgments and feelings around that topic in different ways to help you come up with fresh answers. By taking different perspectives (or wearing many "hats"), you can brainstorm multiple ideas and effectively weigh the viability of each of the solutions you come up with. Or you could use the Crazy 8's or Crazy 9's approach we discussed earlier.

But the most important goal for expanded cognition is to reveal any blindspots or limiting beliefs in your thinking. These limiting beliefs can reflect attitudes about customer preferences, the role of technology, regulation, and the entire basis of competitive differentiation. Because incumbents develop blindspots around these beliefs, it's usually an outsider or upstart startup that sees the tacit opportunity within, and proves that it was all hidden in plain sight.

So how can you learn how to detect a blindspot? You do it by looking for the sacred cow... an industry's foremost belief about value creation. For example, in the taxi business, it's medallions. Then you flip the underlying belief upside down—aka, reframing it—and look for mechanisms to create value. When this works, you'll know because it will take your breath away. Detecting a blindspot is an awakening.

Therefore, when you do your initial design research around blockchains, you must learn how to see beyond your blindspots. You must listen and see more clearly than ever before. When the market gives you feedback, you need to discern between what is and what you are hoping for it to be. This is how you win.

When to Start?

Those born during the Internet era are digital natives, and feel naturally accustomed to exponential rates of change, and are able to absorb multiple streams of high speed information simultaneously. So if you're what I call a "digital immigrant," born in a time when things were linear, you will have a gut instinct only for linear rates of change. Anything faster will seem bewildering. You might think, I'm an immigrant, I'll never catch up. This is absolutely not true.

The only comfort I can provide you is that it gets easier once you jump in. Really, it gets easier. This is because speed is always relative. A useful metaphor is driving. Learning to drive can be frustrating and quite challenging. But once you've made it through the on ramp and the merging process, and everyone is moving at roughly the same speed, the sense of danger and out-of-control velocity diminishes. You enter a state of flow. But to enter that flow, the secret is to accelerate—this empowers you with greater control for the merge. Being afraid to accelerate will only make the onramp more frightening or dangerous. On ramps, motorcycles and skiing... these are all things that are actually safer if you go a bit faster than your comfort zone.

In the early 1900s, the U.S. national speed limit for automobiles was set at 5 mph; only daredevils could drive at speeds like 60 or 70 mph. But people evolve and nowadays, pretty much anyone can drive on a freeway. And many can drive at the maximum speed while putting on makeup or having coffee. Imagine saying that to a race car driver in 1905.

Human beings are evolving every day to adapt to the digital age. Keep this in mind: *it didn't take 100 years for anyone to work his or her way up to 75 mph.* It only took a few months to learn how to drive that fast. The key is that our belief structure has evolved so everyone believes it's doable... so we do it. The same truth holds for enhanced creativity and innovativeness. It will only take a number of months to learn how to innovate at maximum speed. All you have to do is hold the idea that it is not only possible, but that anyone and everyone can do it. And that means you. If you feel that you're too old or not smart enough to develop skills and capacities required for the exponential era... poppycock! Anyone can become a digital native, just as anyone today can learn how to drive faster than the world's greatest racecar driver in 1905.

The other thing you need to do is get out there and practice! The blockchain revolution is already underway, and it's time to learn how to drive on the information superhighway.

Exercises for Chapter XI: Core Creativity

Next time you feel creatively stumped, try some of these creativity boosters:

TASK	DONE	WORKED?	NOTE
Take a hot shower.			
Take a long walk.			An experiment found that "walking increased creativity for 81 percent of participants, with participants increasing their creative output by an average of 60 percent."
Read an inspirational book before bed.			Studies have shown that memory retention increases if sleep "occurs shortly after learning." Take this opportunity to fill up on inspiration, and let your sleeping brain do the rest.
Visualize your problem just before sleeping.			Point your brain in the right direction to subconsciously work on your problem right before sleeping. Don't obsess over it, program it.
Go outside and look at the sky.			A University of British Columbia study found that most people associate blue with openness, peace and tranquility [which] make people feel safe about being creative and exploratory."
Daydream.			A study conducted by researchers from the university of california found that "engaging in simple external tasks that allow the mind to wander may facilitate creative problem solving." Set time aside—maybe even ten minutes a day—to let your mind wander, with no set destination. You may be surprised at where it goes and what you discover. Researchers from the university of california at santa barbara have found that daydreaming when you're consciously aware of what you're doing—called "meta-awareness"—can help you find creative solutions to problems that have been stumping you.
Lie down.			Researchers at the australian national university found that subjects were able to solve problems about 10 percent faster than when standing. Go ahead, get comfortable – just don't fall asleep!
Take a power nap.			But not for too long – around half an hour is good. This is because, while short naps boost your brainpower, entering deep sleep after that stage will cause you to feel groggy when you wake up.

Some additional creativity boosters:

TASK	DONE	WORKED?	NOTE
Work in a new environment.			Same desk, same cup, same computer everyday – not exactly the picture of inspiration. Switch up your working location if you can regularly.
Travel.			"Foreign experiences increase both cognitive flexibility and depth and integrativeness of thought, the ability to make deep connections between disparate forms," says Adam Galinsky, a professor at Columbia Business School. Multi-cultural experiences can make you look at things from other perspectives, and stimulate innovative and flexible thinking, suggests a study in the Journal of Personality and Social Psychology in May 2009.
Work in a coffee shop.			Too much or too little noise may hinder creativity, researchers have found that a moderate hum of background noise may be "just right." In a series of brainstorming experiments published in the Journal of Consumer Research, scientists found that a light level of ambient noise—like you'd find when you settle down with your laptop at Starbucks or Panera—spurred divergent thinking.
Don't tidy your work-space.			A recent experiment by University of Minnesota researchers, which found that "participants in a disorderly room were more creative than participants in an or-derly room." Researchers found that while a neat desk encourages "good behavior," working at a messy desk promoted novel choices and stimulated new ideas.
Doze, but wake your-self just as you fall asleep.			The boundary between sleeping and wak-ing can bring increased creativity.
Take an improv com-edy workshop.			A perfect way to teach yourself how to stretch your imagination at a moment's notice.
Work with a partner you've never worked with before.			Find a new partner, generate ideas on the problematic topic at the same time, then compare notes. You'll almost certainly come across fresh pathways you've never considered before.

To be consistent in training your creative muscles, you need a ritual to center yourself each time – even if you don't feel like it. So design your creativity ritual! What does your daily creativity practice look like? How long is it? Is it fun or all work? Is it alone or with others?

Any human skill, whether its learning to play professional sports or play the piano, requires 5000 hours for the brain to master. Ideation, the skill of creating ideas that solve a central problem, is no different. So make a plan and schedule for how you'll achieve 1000 hours of creativity training.

AMAZON PRICE HISTORY

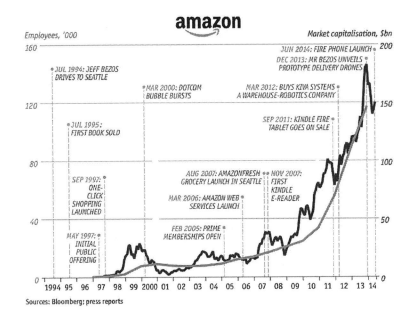

BITCOIN PRICE HISTORY

EERILY SIMILAR?

CHAPTER 12:
THE FUTURE OF BLOCKCHAINS

"The future is here."—Ken Jennings

I REMEMBER ATTENDING A CONFERENCE AUDIENCE IN the late 1990s, back when everyone was complaining that the Internet was being irrationally overhyped. Eric Schmidt, who was then CTO of Sun Microsystems, took the stage and boldly pronounced, "Actually, I think the Internet is being underhyped"... he argued that the true impact of the Internet was going to be greater than we all imagined, and you know, he was right.

If you look at this chart on the previous page that shows the market cap growth for Amazon, you'll see that the dotcom crash was really just a road bump before the long climb into the beautiful digital future. But that bump or pothole... it was the kind that could break your transaxle if you drove over it too fast. On the other hand, if you had given up and stayed out of the market entirely after hitting that bump, you would have missed one of the truly great rides of all time - i.e., if you had invested $10,000 at the IPO, it would be worth about $5 million today. Schmidt put this money where his mouth was, became the CEO of Google, and is now worth north of $10 billion, solidly in three comma territory. The chart showing Bitcoin's history is eerily similar.

It's occurred to me that pretty much the same thing is happening with the blockchain right now. Blockchains are the latest and greatest technology that promise to change the world all over again. However, when addressing the subject, corporate executives need to sound rational and sensible, so they talk about the Gartner hype wave, how the bubble is eventually going to burst, and how we're heading for a "trough of disillusionment." I know Internet pundits who have to play it safe, and talk about how the blockchain is "probably" being overhyped; that it really isn't ready for primetime yet, that it's not secure yet, how it's not scalable yet. They often conflate the blockchain with Bitcoin, and complain that it's like a tulip craze, but without the tulips. But think of this: how is this not like saying in 1999, "Don't invest in Amazon or Google, it's a bubble!"

What's really happening is what Bill Gates said in "The Road Ahead:" "We always overestimate the change that will occur in the next two years and underestimate the change that will occur in the next 10." If you're going to try to make money in 2-3 years off the blockchain revolution, you're probably going to get caught in a correction cycle. But if you're looking to make some money over the next 7-10 years, and looking for a global infrastructural transformation play... the blockchain is probably a pretty good place to give it your best shot

People complain that they are confused about blockchains, that they don't really understand them. But remember, this is just like what happened with the Internet when the Web was in its infancy. Global enterprises were confused about what a web page was, and their full ramification. It took a decade for people to figure it out. But the ones who did sooner, made a lot more money than the ones who didn't. So it's something worth figuring out ASAP. If you're reading this, you probably already know this, and have done your homework.

Cascading Revolutions

For example, here's a peek into the nature of the blockchain technology adoption curve. It's never a smooth ride, a simple linear growth curve all springing from a single invention. Instead, the world experiences a cascade of inventions that add together to form a much bumpier, but steeper curve of societal adoption. For example, the development of the Internet involved the creation of HTML, the subsequent adoption of the browser and the Worldwide Web, the critical mass growth of AOL, Microsoft's adoption of an Internet strategy, the development of Java, the emergence of Google, and so on and so forth.

In the same way, the blockchain revolution will unfold in a similar cascade of interlocking technologies. We project that there will be three waves of technology, each exploding like a mini-big-bang of application development, tools, and functionality. Like the transition from the web to Web 2.0 and then the mobile web, we will see a cascade of development and adoption, each leveraging the technology and installed user base of the previous wave. And just like Thomas Kuhn explained in his book,

"The Structure of Scientific Revolutions," each wave becomes a paradigm that must be broken by the next.

Wave 1 is currently composed of "static ledger apps," that address areas of functionality like remittance, cross-border payment and the correspondent banking system. This arena is already quite frothy, as many banks and insurance companies have invested in requisite technologies. We believe it may already be too late to find early stage investment opportunities in this wave.

However, we're still early for Wave 2, in which applications will focus on "smart contract enabled distributed ledger apps"—or "dapps" in tech shorthand—which can address more complex business processes like trade finance, music royalty management, and IoT application management. You should note that these are very difficult problems to solve, so it may take years to finally arrive at the kinds of applications we anticipate.

Finally, we also believe that there's a Wave 3 of blockchain applications that will emerge shortly. These systems integrate artificial intelligence, optimization and machine learning capabilities to elevate blockchain functionality, but will be so novel that they are unimaginable to most people today. These 'blue ocean' applications are replete with potential for exponential innovation and accelerated collaboration, and can be found in vast undiscovered computational territories that are only now being understood.

For Wave 1, the equivalent of HTML and HTTP will be the core blockchain architecture, which will be supported by the release of ancillary technologies like sharding for scalability. Successful applications will be deployed by companies like Ripple and Circle. Wave 2 will be based on smart contract technology and standards, which will be supported by technologies from Digital Assets Holdings and Ethereum. And for Wave 3, we'll see new emerging standards like DID (decentralized identifiers), blockcerts, and verifiable claims.

Wave 1: Distributed Ledger Apps

Wave 1 blockchain applications will enable the following capabilities:

Dis-intermediation: The blockchain can eliminate middlemen, from brokers to notaries, to reduce the cost of finding, effecting, verifying and settling transactions.

Payment: The blockchain will make it easier and cheaper to make payments, transfer money, or buy and sell goods.

Stored Value: The blockchain can allow you to store money digitally instead of using a bank, money market fund, or government security. It is possible to create smart contracts for treasury bills, to earn interest on your digital holdings, which could make savings accounts obsolete.

Blockchain Lending: You will someday be able to make, secure, settle, and trade loans on the blockchain faster and easier than today.

CyberFunding: Raising money now requires third parties such as investment bankers, venture capitalists, and lawyers—and triggers very expensive regulatory requirements. The blockchain could automate this process and reduce risk so regulatory agencies would eventually embrace them. This will allow enterpreneurs to have greater access to capital than ever before, at the same time reducing risk for investors.

Insuring: The blockchain supports decentralized models for insurance that can make risk management more efficient. This will lower premiums overall.

Accounting: The blockchain enables something called "triple entry accounting," which could make bookkeeping virtually automatic, transparent and instantaneous... enabling an era of "self-auditing" accounting. This will reduce the cost of accounting and CPAs.

Wave 2: Smart Contracts

A perfect example of a Wave 2 blockchain application is in trade finance. First, let's define trade finance: it's when two companies in different countries want to buy and sell from each other. They normally use a bank to guarantee the transaction, and it's a slow and expensive process which hasn't changed much in 400 years. It requires a small mountain of paperwork, and all the parties involved spend a great deal of their time proving that they truly own what they say they own.

Using a blockchain with smart contract capability could significantly transform this $7 trillion industry. For example, in February 2017, a cargo shipment containing $25 million worth of African crude slowly made its way to China. The merchants involved sold and resold the oil three times during the trip. Banks, agents, inspectors, and a commodity trading firm were all involved. The traditional solution involved hundreds of documents and required least three hours to complete each trade.

But on this trip, each trade took less than 25 minutes. The name of the pilot project that made this possible is called Easy Trading Connect. It's a partnership between Société Générale and ING. And it works by moving the transactions to a private version of the Ethereum blockchain.

Saving time wasn't the only benefit of the trade. ING reported that trader efficiency improved by 33% and reduced costs by 30%. Physical documents are prone to human error, fraud, and delays. With the blockchain, all documents get digitized so they're easier and safer to move around. And it solves a lot of paperwork problems. Further, they were able to "auto-check" documents on a computer rather than doing it manually. Experts now estimate the blockchain will cut trade finance costs up to $20 billion.

This trade finance example allows us to better understand the functionality and impact of Wave 2 blockchain applications, and how they could lead to a substantial reduction in paperleading, to finally manifest to realizing the dream of the paperless office, reducing costs, speeding transactions, and insuring greater trade security.

Wave 3: Next Generation Blockchain

As an example of what a next generation blockchain application would look like, let me briefly describe a pilot application I'm working on, that proposes to transform innovation in vaccine research by enabling large-scale collaborative efforts to be managed via a number of interoperating blockchains. This venture proposes to use blockchain technology to incentivize access to, and rapid dissemination of, pathogenic information in the arena of infectious disease research. What's the potential benefit for this system? The upside for society could be preventing the next major pandemic!

But to make this happen, the system needs to built using a network of interacting blockchain applications that manage intellectual property, royalty licensing for IP developed through the system, potential equity ownership in tech spinoffs, and a new way to manage trust in a full decentralized Internet—something we call "trust objects" and "verifiable claims." The blockchains that manage IP would enable expanded and empowered collaboration. The royalty tracking distributed ledger would simplify and improve IP licensing. The cyber-equity blockchain would not only improve research in life sciences, but could also transform how life science venture accelerators increase their effectiveness and reach in general. As a side benefit, they could change the way Initial Cybertoken Offerings are executed.

Trust objects are decentralized, encapsulated trust datagrams that are exchanged by business partners and rely on verifiable claims technology, and can be used to create an infrastructure for a global "trustworthiness index." For example, a certified financial planner would get trust objects from the university he studied at, the governmental entity that certified him, the bonding agency that provided a bond, and all the customers who provided positive digital references—all of these would reside on the blockchain, and would enable an eco-system of trust for the business network and multiple parties could help rate and manage trust objects. This can be applied to vaccine research, licesning and production. For example, if a number of parties wish to license your technology, shouldn't you know their reputation for timely payment of licensing royalties?

Furthermore, using Trust Objects would enable the ability to "transactionalize" the search process to turn a blockchain into a marketplace. Again, we call this process the marketization of blockchains; this will be the hallmark of Wave 3 applications. Add the ability too improve the fundraising process for startups, via ICOs, making it both easier for companies and safer for investors. All of this would lead to a new framework for innovation—an open empowered innovation smart grid powered by the IP blockchain.

The transformation of the global innovation process could possibly result in exponential value growth, by bringing participants into the eco-system who create additional, new assets that can benefit others beyond original participant group. The result is shared value creation, as the eco-system itself becomes something of intangible value that benefits its participants in new ways.

What's the impact of all of this? Well, if we could transform the centuries old patent system, it could improve core innovation processes and potentially speed the development of a global innovation smart grid. Since the majority of high paying jobs are created by startups, improving core innovation process by just 5-10% would equate to lifting global job creation by nearly an equal rate. Access to capital would also lift innovative capacity globally.

But all of this is just scratching the surface of what is possible. Third generation blockchain applications could produce equally disruptive transformations in every sector of the global economy, from music production to media distribution, from marketing to sales, from healthcare to insurance to the Internet of Things.

One thing is for sure: the full potential of Wave 3 blockchains is breathtaking, and likely to reshape the world in dramatic and unforeseeable ways.

Exercises for Chapter 12: The Future

1) *What ideas do you have for third generation functionality?*

2) *How would a third generation blockchain application change the world?*

3) What needs to happen to make it possible to create third generation blockchain application?

4) How would you market it? How would it market itself?

5) Who would be the ideal governance partner for a third generation blockchain application?

6) What timeframe do you think it'll happen in?

NEXT: A QUANTUM LEAP INTO YOUR FUTURE

"Jump, and you will find out how to unfold your wings as you fall."
—Ray Bradbury

THIS QUOTE HAS BEEN ATTRIBUTED TO Charles Darwin: "It is not the strongest of the species that survives, nor the most intelligent. It is the one that is the most adaptable to change." This is as true for human beings as it is for any other species. And if you think about it, innovation is built into the genes of the human species, because of the innate human capacity for reflection, change, creativity, invention, and transformation.

The challenge has been amplified by the fact that in today's world, change is most decidedly accelerating. In the not-too-distant future, a jarring shift from linear to exponential change will occur, and when it does, it will unleash something humanity has no experiential "gut" instinct for. When this shift happens, success will belong to those rare people and organizations that have not only the capacity to adapt to change, but thrive in it. In fact, the most successful will be those who are most adept at creating disruptive change... for everyone else to worry about. Mastering disruption keeps your competitors off balance and struggling to catch up.

The enormous change that is coming will dwarf the change we have already experienced, which has already significantly transformed the world over the last three decades. The digital revolution has enabled a miraculous 98% reduction in the cost of computing and communication during this time period. Also, it wasn't a single wave of change, because technological change comes in something physicists call wave trains, that add up into a tsunami. What we've seen during the digital revolution so far has only been the first series of wavelets in a larger framework of complete and overwhelming societal transformation. And so, another order of magnitude reduction in the cost of computing and communications is coming straight at us like a freight train. This is roughly equivalent to taking all of the power of every supercomputer in the world today, and stuffing it into your child's videogame machine in 20-30 years.

At the bleeding edge of this coming tsunami is the blockchain. Plain old linear thinking and "best practices"—that are good for dealing with static business process—are simply not up to the task of managing the kind of disruption that we're facing as we are hit by the full brunt of the distributed ledger and its potential for disrupting business models.

Therefore, the goal for this book has been to help you develop a map for surviving the coming disruption and dislocation... and for achieving success in the digital age. What's really great is that by learning how to thrive, and by joining the blockchain revolution. To do this, you must overcome the dominant paradigm of resignation and inertia. Thus, my hope is that this book will not only help you survive the blockchain revolution, but to create the life of your dreams... and to build a better tomorrow for everyone by doing so.

Thus, this book combines techniques for Agile innovation, new skills to increase your innovative potential, with exercises that are focused on actually building a blockchain. These are the action steps that are required to make your vision a reality.

One last thing—this book is written for both people who are slow to embrace the digital revolution, as well as those already immersed in the leading edge of it. But the key is this: as motivational philosopher Jim Rohn has so aptly put it, "You can't hire someone else to do your push-ups for you."

This is the simple truth—you've got to do your own pushups, if you are to get any value out of them. Whether that means innovating, exercising, reading, studying, meditating, learning a new computer or human language, participating in a success circle, setting measurable goals, or designing your killer app blockchain business plan... you are going to have to put in the effort yourself. No one else can do these things for you. This is why this is a workbook, so you can do the work!

Good luck!

finis

APPENDIX A: AN ICO PRIMER

INITIAL COIN OFFERINGS HAVE RAISED OVER a billion dollars for early stage startups in the past year. And they've done it with remarkable blinding speed: Status.im, a browsing/messaging app, raised $100 million in under three hours. Brave, a browser startup launched by former CEO of Mozilla, raised $35 million in under 30 seconds. Tezos raised an impressive $232 million over 12 days with an uncapped ICO. A new era of startup financing is dawning. So many of you, especially those who have spent close to a year raising a round of angel or venture capital, are probably watching with slack jaws or tongues hanging... the question is "how can I get in on this action?"

Please note that the blockchain is central to the business models of most startups that use ICOs. By distributing tokens in an ICO, a startup gives buyers early access to its technology, to use however they see fit. If the service or product catches on—or in some cases, before it even launches—the buyers could sell their tokens for a profit on secondary markets. Even companies that are not blockchain-centric are getting into the act: Kik, a message service founded way back in 2009, is using the blockchain to spruce up its business model... it plans to conduct an ICO later this year. The pipeline is filling up rapidly.

It looks like a "benestrophe"—all the factors are magically lining up the right way: speculators' appetites for blockchain investments rapidly expanding, leading venture capitalists like Chris Dixon of Andreessen Horowitz and Fred Wilson of Union Square Ventures are saying that ICOs are the next big thing; promising companies are emerging to stage ICOs. The startup, meanwhile, raises money without surrendering control to venture capitalists, and without the costs and regulatory burdens of an equity IPO.

So here how it happens: First, an ICO is not unlike a crowdfunding campaign. So what you do, typically, is start a company and build some shareholder value so it looks like a promising early stage startup—a great concept and an open beta to show people. Then, you announce your plan to launch a token sale, and publish a white paper about what you intend to create, how you intend to do it, and how much money you need to make it happen. Then, you launch your new cryptocurrency on CoinList or Waves, which promises to "create your blockchain token in one minute." Finally, you press the button and launch your initial coin offering.

Sounds simple huh? Well, it's not quite as simple as that. What's happening today is that while the early entrants are experiencing runaway success, and everyone thinks its going to be a cakewalk to make millions, the reality is that fortune favors the bold. In this case, the companies that were first to market were lucky enough to get "fluke hits" – and everyone else out there is part of a very large crowd of companies all about to start screaming for attention. The other shoe to drop is a recent crash in cryptocurrency prices, which was partially caused by all the ICO's trying to cash out on Ethereum, and leading to significant sell-side pressure. All of this will be figured out by the market, but going forward, you can't just cookie-cutter an ICO, you have to understand what you're doing explicitly and execute flawlessly to even have a chance at success.

It is very likely that some form of ICO could be the future of investing, a transformative approach to fundraising that enables consumers to benefit more directly from the popularity of new technologies than they would if they owned a traditional stock. And also, the process cuts out the middle man so it's more upside to share between investor and startup. Finally, the Achilles heel of venture capital has been that investments are typically illiquid for several years. The possibility of investing in a venture fund that enjoys virtually immediate liquidity is absolutely revolutionary.

Critics, meanwhile, rightfully worry that ICOs are in a regulatory grey zone that could leave investors defenseless against fraud and could possibly land startups in significant legal hot water down the line. However, the U.S. Securities and Exchange Commission is generally reluctant to use a heavy hand, lest it stifle innovation and the benefits that it can bring. On the other hand, when investors start losing money on ICOs and the lawsuits begin, the SEC will start singing a different tune.

That tune has already begun, with the Commission issuing a cautionary notice in late July 2017, that securities law "may apply" to token sales in some circumstances. Going forward, this means that companies issuing tokens as part of an ICO may need to register with the commission. This will force companies to comply with regulations that ask them to reveal their financial position and the identities of their management. This is actually a good thing, in that it will bring balance to the industry.

By issuing a warning, but not filing charges, it simply put every ICO on notice that they will no longer be handing out free passes. This will inevitably elevates the standards for ICOs and protect investors, which will usher in a new era of "tempered innovation" that foster will sustainable development. This is better in the long run, as it will force companies to focus more on its competency and innovative technology, and less on disguising financial instruments to skirt the law. Emin Gun Sirer, a Cornell professor who studies blockchains, has said that this is not the beginning of the end for ICOs, it is the "end of beginning for blockchains."

Also, because this is a global innovation, dampening enthusiasm for ICOs in the United States will inevitably increase interest in pursuing them overseas. Expect to see exchanges in other countries pick up the slack. The flip side of the ruling is that it quietly begins to legitimize blockchain technology for financial instruments, putting Wall Street on notice that blockchains are definitely coming.

Also, in its ruling, the agency also suggested that it is looking for a way to encourage the promise of blockchain-based financial innovation, while also protecting investors from scammers. The Chairman of the SEC stated, "The SEC is studying the effects of distributed ledger and other innovative technologies and encourages market participants to engage with us. We seek to foster innovative and beneficial ways to raise capital, while ensuring – first and foremost – that investors and our markets are protected." So this is actually a major opportunity for "compliance-savvy" innovation.

The Mechanics of ICOs

Here's what happens in an ICO: A company releases a certain number of crypto-tokens and then sells those tokens to its intended audience. As a result, the company gets the capital to fund the product development and the audience members get their "tokens."

How tokens operate is rather ingenious. For example, consider Storjcoins, which were released by Storj.io during its ICO. Storj.io is a decentralized cloud storage startup, and when its main product is released the users will be able to spend Storjcoins (purchased at a discount) on the storage space they will offer, in addition to just being able to trade them like any other coin. See how their tokens fit into the business model? Another prominent example is Ethereum, a platform for building decentralized applications of all kinds. The company's tokens called "ethers" are actively used to maintain the operation of apps that have already been built upon the platform. The spectrum of possible uses depends on the scope of the project.

In most cases, the crypto-tokens released during an ICO are sold at a fixed price denominated in bitcoins, ethers or US dollars. That price isn't backed by anything but the community's faith in the development team to actually finish and release the product at some point in the future, so it's usually pretty low. After the project is completed and launched, the tokens' value will be secured by a real, working product, that almost always leads to an increase in price. When this happens, the original backers could sell their tokens for a substantial profit. For example, during the ICO of Ethereum in 2014, the tokens were sold at a price ranging from 30¢ to 40¢ per token. After the project's main platform was released in July 2015, the price of each token rose significantly, reaching as high as $19.42 at one point. This means that some of the early investors were able to claim an ROI of over 6000%!

How is an ICO different from an IPO?

There are a number of parallels between the concepts of Initial Public Offering and an Initial Coin Offering. However, at the same time, there are some important differences. For one, a company's shares, released during an IPO, always denote a share of ownership in the respective company. This is not, by default, a case with crypto-tokens that are sold to the public in an ICO. Crypto-tokens can be used to transfer voting powers - a larger share of tokens giving more voting power - in some projects, but more often those tokens are just that - units of currency that you can send to other users and exchange for other currencies.

The other crucial difference is that IPO's are heavily regulated by the government. Due to regulatory changes, such as the 2002 Sarbanes-Oxley Act (SOX), the IPO process has become an intensely arduous and increasingly expensive ordeal. These days, companies going public should expect to pay more than $2 million in out of pocket expenses to cover a host of fees—among them legal, accounting, printing, listing, filing—in addition to the underwriter discount and commission of 7 percent of the offering proceeds and to shore up internal processes to meet the tougher reporting and governance standards for public companies. There are also severe consequences in the case of non-compliance.

Conversely, cryptocurrency crowdfunding is a new scene, which government regulatory bodies are maintaining a hands-off approach... at least until people start losing money. That means that any project that can launch an ICO at any time with little preparation and any person can take part in it and contribute their money, no matter what country they are from. This liberal environment carries both new opportunities and risks when compared to the more conservative IPO's.

It's important to remember that ICO campaigns are not suitable for every business. They may actually be detrimental to some companies: you will spend time and money on a campaign, only to fail in securing enough funds. And the formative days, when all you had to do was publish a white paper, are behind us now. Today, you need to know how to do it right, otherwise you'll be lost in a sea of other half-baked ICOs. This is just like with crowdfunding, the early experimenters won big, and now, but now, over 2000 crowdfunding sites are hosting hundreds of thousands of campaigns, and only a small percentage are raising millions of dollars. And those are ones who executed flawlessly.

There are certain informal requirements for both ICO and crowdfunding campaigns, that I have merged into a single set of emerging success factors. These include: (i) generating true value and utility for the users, (ii) authenticity and transparency, (iii) proactively implement investor protection functionality, (iv) the integration of the token, sold during the crowdsale, organically into your product's core functionality, (v) integrated viral dynamics, and (vi) resilience against speculative pressure as soon as it hits the markets.

How to Prepare for an Initial Coin Offering

It's really important to get the ICO right, because it's not just about raising the money. If you intelligently integrate of the token, sold during the crowdsale, organically into your product's core functionality, it will help in gaining initial market penetration as well. Plus, it removes the middleman in startup funding, so more money goes to the startup and more return to the investor or angels. Finally, it provides the public market's unofficial stamp of approval on the concept.

So here are the five steps to take to insure a successful ICO:

Step 1: Pre-announcement Validation

Right now, an ICO pre-campaign generally consists of making announcements of the future project in the various communities of cryptocurrency investors (see table X). The founders of the project write an executive summary – essentially a small presentation to investors, in which they explain the essence and purpose of the ICO project. After the executive summary, the company receives the first feedback, which can be analyzed to see whether the project could interest investors or not. The pre-announcement may cause many questions about the business model of the project and unperceived risks. Taking into account all incoming comments, the business model receives proper adjustments. This feedback process with subsequent adjustments is repeated for several cycles, as long as there is no agreement between the founders and prospective investors. The first stage ends with making the final business model of the project and writing the detailed offer.

I believe that in the next stage of ICO evolution, you'll have to do a bit more than this. I believe that companies will need to bite the bullet and write offering documents that include a prospectus, that includes financials, risks, and full transparency of the business strategy.

It starts with coming up with a compelling "story." Crafting the right unique value proposition and an intelligent marketing strategy in the prospectus is critical to the success of the ICO. It's really about strategically positioning your company—highlighting its strengths, strategy, the market opportunity, and investment précis. Also, learning from crowdfunding, that story needs to generate emotional resonance, so consider producing a compelling video—which is considered vital for crowdfunding campaigns.

Kickstarter.com reports that projects including a video get successfully funded 50% of the time, while those without are only 30% likely to fund their project, and raise significantly more money too. So it would make sense to consider the inclusion of an impactful video. Please note that the crowdfunding videos that have helped raise the most funds, are not the ones that go crazy on Hollywood production values. The videos that work the best are modest and direct, and simply say, "this is us, and we're not hiding anything." More importantly, they allow you to present your passion honestly.

Remember, people never invest in an idea; they invest in a person. Use simple and clear language that gives a honest and concise portrayal of who you really are, as real people. And more importantly, show that your passion is real and worth supporting.

Second, you need to generate some decent financials, even if you don't have any financial history, because it shows you have the ability to report regularly going forward. So put an effort into insuring that the proper systems are in place to ensure a flow of accurate, timely accounting information—which I recommend to be released at least annually, or perhaps quarterly. You don't need to ramp up to a Sarbanes-Oxley level of audited reporting, known as the 10-K and 10-Q, just make a genuine effort to show that

ensure that information is properly captured for the company's reporting to investors and token holders. It's more important to identify the right metrics and closely monitor them to enhance your business results, since it forces everyone in the company to focus on the key factors that drive your business.

Third, this is your last chance to spruce up the management team—especially if your spouse forced you to hire your brother-in-law, whose only experience in marketing is selling used cars. Also, the management team should show some financial and accounting experience. And, it is important that key managers possess strong communication skills to present the company's vision and its performance to the market, and to meet the often-intensive informational demands

Here is a list of some of the more popular Bitcoin discussion forums for your reference:

- Bitcoins.net
- Bitcoin.com
- NewsBtc.com
- Blockchainews.com
- Cryptocoinsnews.com
- Coinspot.io
- Coinspeaker.com
- Forklog.com
- Bits.media
- BTCManager.com

FIGURE 9: FORUMS

of research analysts and investors. Finally, if you don't have a formal board of directors, this is a good time to form one.

You'll also be able to considering hiring the equivalent of an investment bank, to help you through the process. If so, you can stage a "beauty contest." You invite three to five of these companies to make presentations to your board about how they see the company, how to structure and price your token, what they expect to see in the current market, and why they are the firm that should underwrite the offering.

After you begin the ICO process, you should observe something similar to the SEC's restriction called a 'quiet period', which significantly limits what you can say and do after registering for an IPO. You must likewise be vigilant in controlling the kind of information to insure you aren't accused of a "pump and dump" scheme. In general, the SEC is interested in insuring transparency around the factors, assumptions, and methodologies used to determine pricing, so you should do likewise. By "self-compiling" in a decentralized way, we can insure the growth of ICOs as a community.

Step 2: Creating the Offer

The token offer covers all the nuances of the project, specifies the desired amount of investments, plans and project deadlines, and the operational functionality of the tokens.

You should also speak with a number of prospective ICO investors, and maybe form a pricing committee. The final pricing usually occurs right before the ICO is launched to account for any last minute shifts in the market.

A token can be equal, for example, to $1.00 of a debt, 1 share of the company, 10 shares of the company, the right to vote anywhere else, whatever you want. No established standards on what will be the token in a particular project, so it is specified individually in each offer. After selecting a financial instrument, the offer covers all the rights possessed by the token. For example, ETH token, released during ICO Ethereum was of extremely speculative nature, and DGD token in addition to being backed by foreign exchange reserves, also gives the holder the right to put forward proposals for the management of the company to the other shareholders.

Again, you need to show that your team, the goals and the protection of investors' interests are paramount. A great team behind the project is probably the most important factor when investors decide on contributing to an ICO. Thus, you must list all major team members, along with their faces and social media profiles, openly available to any potential contributor. Also, you should avoid suffering major team shifts in the period right before and during the campaign: it could cause a drop in investors confidence and result in underperformance of your ICO.

Next, make sure that your goals are clearly defined and realistic. Unrealistic or unclear goals are the kiss of death, because they make an impression that the team either doesn't know what it's doing or, worse still, is trying to actively scam people out of their money. Thus, you need to have a white paper, a roadmap and ideally a prospectus prepared before the launch of an ICO. The white paper has to clearly outline the technical aspects of the product, the problems it intends to solve and how it is going to solve them. Likewise, the roadmap has to list clearly defined and realistically achievable goals and their timeframes. The prospectus should provide the entire business case, along with financials and a clear articulation of risks.

Frankly, for an ICO, the very best thing you could do is show a proof of concept. Being able to present a working code to the audience is the best thing you could wish for when preparing for an ICO. If that is the case, it is strongly advisable to make the prototype the main focus of the campaign. You can take a look at the Humaniq ICO, which is a good example of a well thought-out campaign. A detailed whitepaper and roadmap, clearly defined goals for the project, commentary from independent expert and developers happy to reveal their identities - these are all signs of a legitimate campaign.

Now about investor protections... there are effectively no guarantees enforced by the government, so companies doing ICOs should self-impose restrictions on themselves to provide sufficient trust and transparency for the contributors. For example, you can store the contributions of the community members in escrow wallets. And obviously, you need to establish a legal entity for the company and document the terms and conditions of the ICO.

Next, in general, early bird discounts for investors which contribute in the first few days of the campaign are a must. We can learn from crowdfunding on Kickstarter or Indiegogo— early investors need to get a better deal. That provides an incentive for early adopters, who then generate momentum for a larger number of investors to follow. It also helps to generate positive PR and social chatter, all of which can create a groundswell of activity that will make your ICO successful.

Another convention which has by now become a de facto requirement is collecting all contribution in a multi-signature escrow wallet, with all the names of all key holders announced to the public. Some of those keys have to be held by people otherwise uninvolved in your project, which serves as an additional guarantee for investors' funds safety. But be careful in the selection of the multi-signature wallet technology, as these have been hacked in the past. You should also make sure that there is a process in place for the returning of the funds to their contributors - there is always a possibility that you will fail to reach the targets and will be forced to roll the campaign back.

Finally, it's good to join an ICO platform, so you can get more traffic and PR coverage, much like Kickstarter or Indiegogo does for crowdfunding. Some of them: Waves, ICONOMI, State of the Dapps. The Waves Platform is one of the largest such platforms. It allows anyone - for example, a young blockchain startup - to set up a digital token in mere minutes and at almost no cost. These tokens can then be listed on

Waves' own exchange - to be easily found by eager investors. This allows the company to secure the necessary funding.

Step 3: Building the Outreach Platform

Before the process of selling and buying tokens begins, you need to implement a PR campaign. Since ICOs are often carried out for young and little-known companies, an important role in the success of the project requires a successful PR strategy.

Getting enough attention is actually one of the hardest tasks for ICOs, as the market is growing rapidly and there is an ICO launch almost every day. Make sure to constantly communicate with your audience both before and throughout the campaign. This will help get more people on board, as well as provide feedback, allowing you to tweak while the ICO is underway. The main channels of communication here are the social media - Twitter and Facebook and Reddit, and the aforementioned Bitcoin discussion forums. Consider the option of hiring a professional whose only job will be to monitor and participate in the dialogue with your audience on those websites - there's nothing worse than having a well-prepared campaign fail simply due to the lack of outreach.

For IPOs, what hopeful companies do is called a "Road Show." It is a series of meetings with prospective major investors and analysts in key cities around the world, which lasts from two to four weeks and is focused not only on institutionalized investors (banks, pension funds, etc.), but on a broad segment of smaller investors.

An ICO road show can be implemented using webinar technology. For an ICO, you must focus on both "Bitcoin whales" and "business angels." Such investors can not only get things started, but are compelling social connectors who can propel your message virally. If you can get a celebrity investor, like a well known venture capitalist, that would be a definite plus.

What I recommend is a process I call "rumble, lightning, thunder." You have to start with a rumble, before the campaign starts, and sign up hundreds of people to commit the instant you launch. It's a lot like a book getting released – if the initial sales are strong, its success is a self-fulfilling prophecy. It's important to gather your instant liftoff community before you launch. And when you launch, you have to execute like lightning. Flawlessly. Without a hiccup. If you're fast out of the gate, the bloggers will want to report about you. You go to the top of the "what's hot" list. Herd behavior sets in and it's all to your benefit. That's the thunder stage, when the herd starts stampeding toward your campaign.

Thus, the key learning from the crowdfunding world is that it's really all about building your community and outreach platform. It's said that the three most important keys to succeeding with crowdfunding are community, community and community. You need a solid core team of hard workers who can help manage daily promotion, and personally thanking token purchasers. It is vital to "pre-rally" a large group of people who are eager to commit to help you and relay your tweets and posts, the minute the ICO campaign goes live. If you hope to accumulate millions of dollars in investment, you need a launch team of approximately 100 people who are willing to step up and actively help you get the word out to at least 100,000 potential investors.

Finally, you need to reward the community that provides you with a platform. This is pretty obvious to most people already, but it's amazing how many campaigns forget to do this.

Step 4: Launch the ICO Successfully

There are two ways to release the token on blockchain: In the first way, you can first collect a minimum amount of money, specified by the offer, and then release the tokens and divide them among investors in proportion. For this purpose usually a special site with the investor's office is organized, for example chronobank.io. The second way is to sell the token on the cryptocurrency exchanges. To this end, it is necessary to release it in advance that allows trading them on one or several exchanges simultaneously. In this case, the ICO process becomes very similar to the traditional IPO process.

If you're lucky, your ICO will be fully subscribed in less than a day. But it's more likely, with the forthcoming flood of ICO offers, that it will require a longer offering period.

Step 5: Life after the ICO

Once you complete the offering, you must begin acting like a public company. It's good discipline and can help insure success. The most important task is to follow through on your promises to be open and transparent, to work diligently on executing the strategy effectively, and to report on progress in a regular and reliable manner. At the very least, you should offer the equivalent of an annual report to token holders, and perhaps quarterly reports as well. All of this will maintain investor confidence.

Do not underestimate the considerable effort that must be expended to maintain your market position. If investor enthusiasm for a company is not maintained, trading will decline. If a company's shares are thinly traded, the benefits sought from the ICO (including the use of the token to insure the success of your business model) will not be realized. Thus, effective distribution and support of the token, as well as continuing token analyst interest, is necessary after the ICO.

A strategy for after-market support usually includes choosing an individual within a company to handle token-holder relations. This helps to ensure that your company will release information that is uniform and accurate. Unless someone is directly responsible for this, it may fall through the cracks as things get busy.

In the case of a new venture, earnings are the key factor that affects the public's perception of a company... it's innovation capacity. Your company should project a positive image about your innovation capacity to your investors, token holders, customers, and community. You should issue regular reports about how committed your management is, how your solution is being perceived by customers in pilot trials, new strategic partners you've brought into the fold.

Also, there is growing interest regarding corporate social responsibility, including sustainability and climate change issues, so don't be shy about expressing your commitment to social change.

Finally, you need to realize that most of your funding will be in the form of cryptocurrency, and it would be difficult to convert to fiat currency without tanking the price of ether or whatever. For example, Tezos raised $220 million in four days, but when Bitcoin went down in value, it dropped to $142 million, even as the company continued to raise. As Bitcoin recovered, the amount went back up...but the risk remains.

Understanding Risks

As long as we're on the subject of risks, very few people genuinely understand how to regulate the processes taking place within the cryptocurrency market. The virtual economy, carrying out all its transactions via Internet payment, without direct contact of the seller and the buyer is always fraught with risks. The ICO is no exception.

According to experts, the majority of the existing projects up to 2017 may turn out to be fraudulent, because no one conducted a quality due diligence effort— an in-depth analysis of an investment object in the form of a report. The analysis includes an assessment of investment risks, a thorough investigation of the company, a comprehensive review of its financial condition and market position, expertise and previous experience of the attracting team.

In case of cryptocurrency economy and ICO, due diligence is often conducted cursorily, which leads to investment in projects that are not backed by a real business. We can see this on the example of equity crowdfunding of all kinds of lotteries and casinos. To protect the depositors, by analogy with the traditional financial market, new players have emerged on the cryptocurrency market, i.e., rating agencies like ICORating.

These agencies conduct independent due diligence, make analysis of all the information about the company, entering the cryptocurrency exchange, and publish the results of their research in the form of an independent rating review indicating the strong and weak points of projects. To minimize the risk of investors, companies that provide the services on launching ICO, cooperate with rating agencies.

A rating agency will conduct research of all aspects of the project: the business model, the market dynamics, the team (including blockchain-development experience), the competition, technical background, and an analysis of the feedback from the community.

Also, there are risks to the company! The biggest downside to doing a reputable ICO is the pressure to deliver quarterly reports and investor management, which sometimes detracts from focusing on getting the product completed and launched. Also, an ICO may force certain companies to reveal sensitive information that a fully private company would not have to reveal. In a worst-case scenario, a group of dissident token investors could make a lot of trouble for you. And if the token performs poorly after a company the ICO, even though your product is coming along nicely, it could generate negative publicity or "an anti-marketing event" for the company.

ICOs and Venture Capitalists

Some people are saying that ICOs are the Uber of the venture capital business, that ICOs will replace venture capitalists. As of early June, blockchain-related startups have raised $327 million through ICOs, more than the $295 million blockchain entrepreneurs have raised through VC funding, according to CoinDesk.

At the same time, some VCs have been testing the idea of raising funds themselves with ICOs. At a recent CB Insights panel, Satya Patel, cofounder of seed-stage venture firm Homebrew, floated the idea of raising the firm's next fund in an ICO, saying it had even been discussed among the partners. It must be remembered that liquidity is a huge advantage of ICOs. Venture investments can be tied up for years before seeing a return, while markets in bitcoin, ether and other cryptocurrencies allow for immediate trades of any currency purchased in an ICO.

A key data point to consider is that the most successful ICOs have been tied to an influential VC: Tezos and Bancor, two of the biggest ICOs yet, were backed by legendary investor Tim Draper. A number of other VCs have stepped into the space, including San Francisco venture firm Blockchain Capital (which $10 million in six hours) and Andreessen Horowitz and Union Square Ventures (which put $10 million into Polychain).

This suggests that the more agile VCs will simply evolve faster to take advantage of ICOs to claw their way up higher in the VC food chain. What is likely to happen is that companies could use an ICO as a seed round – replacing the angel investor – and then be better positioned to raise venture capital or do an IPO later. And a strong ICO would mean founders could negotiate from a position of strength in a venture capital round later.

Therefore, a company that has already raised cash in an ICO could focus on finding a more productive relationship with the right VC rather than being forced to partner with a VC who will provide the greatest amount of capital.

Also, in order to de-risk their investments, VCs often prefer not provide all of the capital in a round. This means bringing in other VCs who may not add as much business support, networking, and advisory. If the startup has cash from an ICO, a VC is less likely to need to bring in partners that don't add much value but demand a higher valuation.

We are at the very beginning of the history of blockchains, and ICOs are a way for all of us to participate in that future. Venture capitalists see this and will find a way to co-exist in this new world.

Wrapping it Up

In conclusion, we would like to note that the rapidly developing blockchain-economy and growing ICO market repeats the history of formation and development of the traditional stock exchange market, but at warp speed.

Some of the projects that are currently carrying out ICO have the capacity to eventually grow to an enormous size, and repeatedly return the investments put. Many investors today remember the time of entering IPO by companies such as Apple, Amazon or Google and assess what capital they could have earned, if they had invested in these companies at that time. Today ICO market provides another chance to participate in the success stories of the new economy projects, both for investors and for companies whose founders want to create really important projects.

What we need to do is work together to insure that investors can enjoy more reliable, understandable and effective ICOs and projects - reducing risks, maximizing the potential profits, increasing market transparency and stability. And that starts with you!

APPENDIX B: CREATIVITY NEURO-PATHWAYS

ONE FINAL PARTING GIFT TO YOU, dear Reader, is a method to discover and map your innovative strengths. Most innovation experts classify innovation skill sets these categories--you're either a visionary, a maker, or a coach/facilitator, this is different. This approach has to do with how your brain is wired, and is similar to something called the Five Love Languages, a book by Gary Chapman that outlines five ways to express and experience love. These map to whether our brain process is primarily visual, auditory, or somatic—so the languages map roughly to the five senses. The love languages are: words of affirmation, acts of service, receiving gifts, quality time, and physical touch.

It's a great book that has helped countless couples. It's pretty simple concept--if you are auditory primary, then your love language is "words of affirmation" and you really need to hear someone say they love you. If they try to give you gifts or acts of service, it doesn't really connect. You have to connect via the particular neural pathway of your beloved.

The five pathways to innovativeness and business creativity are:
- *Enhanced Listening*
- *Visual Thinking*
- *Devotional Creativity*
- *Mental Focus*
- *Kinesthetic prototypes*

So, in a way similar to love languages, those wishing to access greater creativity should seek to do so using their dominant neural pathway for creativity.

If you are really into music and love to chat with friends over coffee, maybe you're auditory primary. If so, focus on active listening and building ethnographic interviewing skills. This will help you to detect pain points more effectively, which will unearth the aha's that power innovation.

If you're a painter, photographer or can't think without a whiteboard, maybe you're visual primary. If so, keep using that whiteboard, get a sketchbook to doodle innovation notes, and focus on building your visual thinking skills. This will help you to collaborate and see the big picture more effectively.

If you are the type of person who is moved emotionally, and cry at the movies or believe in causes, then devotional creativity might be right for you. Seek a muse or a cause, and let that fill you with the energy to succeed. Focus on what you love.

If you enjoy a strong ability to maintain mental focus, turn work into a meditation and build "zenergy" to achieve deeper focus and productivity. This means you can figure out the hardest problems, just keep focused and unstoppable in your drive.

If you are shamelessly hedonistic, or maybe a bit of a massage junkie, perhaps your creativity is kinesthetically activated. If so, learn how to innovate with your hands, and build prototypes and systems.

And of course, if you can't decide what you pathway into creativity is, then try them all and see what works. As human beings, we are wired to use all our senses, so all of these approaches are valid for you to try. Just do what works.

APPENDIX C: ABOUT FUTURELAB

AT FUTURELAB, WE WORK WITH OUR clients to co-create robust strategies and processes to support sustained, long-term success in the complex and rapidly-changing world. By design, our organization is a hybrid of a consulting firm and a technology developer, which enables us to bring advanced insights to our clients, while client insights help to guide the design of our technology platforms.

Principles of Innovation

As consultants, our clients range from Global 500 companies to national governments to major international humanitarian agencies, and even museums. We have helped them develop and implement key strategies, innovation management systems, apply technology to reach a global workforce with leading edge information, training, and tools, and helped to define their future organizations.

Throughout all of our projects we apply principles that have been carefully developed and proven across a wide range of instances. A key fundamental principle for innovation success is the implementation of the "innovation portfolio," a collection of initiatives and investments that address varying markets with varying risk profiles. Designing and managing portfolios is indeed a strategy for managing and mitigating risk, and since innovation is by definition inherently risky, thoughtful portfolio strategies are essential. While no one can be sure which initiatives will succeed, the odds of overall success improve significantly when we diversify intelligently.

Another important principle is reflected in the value of creating a "base platform" of core capabilities from which and upon which specific applications for various users and markets can be mounted. FutureLab has invested in developing such a platform, a robust "industrial grade" technology platform whose extensive functionality is an ideal foundation upon which to build a broad portfolio of blockchain applications.

The FutureLab Technology Platform

FutureLab technologies support innovation in enterprises, and reflect a deep understanding of the ways that well- designed tools for idea generation and idea management can support large organizations. Our innovation platform, OS/i, the Operating System for Innovation, is a comprehensive innovation management tool for small, medium, and large-sized enterprises.

We have significantly expanded this core feature set to include critical tools for executive management of extensive innovation initiatives through portfolio management, executive dashboards, and strategic alignment through future disruption mapping.

We've also develop AI and machine learning capabilities to augment and simplify the analysis of large data sets, as well as simulation and modeling tools, optimization algorithms.

To assure that our work was based on solid conceptual frameworks and rigorously documented, we prepared the landmark books *Agile Innovation* (Wiley, 2014), *Foresight and Extreme Creativity* (FutureLab, 2016), and *The Agile Innovation Master Plan* (FutureLab, 2017).

FutureLab and the Blockchain

As we studied the bitcoin and blockchain phenomena we realized that the qualities and characteristics that make for an effective innovation management tool are also integral aspects of the blockchain value proposition. Trust, identity, verification, and ownership of assets are all issues that arise when we deal with innovations and innovators who wish to collaborate to advance their ideas, but who hesitate to share indiscriminately for fear of losing the value of their IP.

Consequently, we have begun to build blockchain capabilities directly into our innovation management solution, and as we are the first or among the first to do so, it seems that we now have a market-leading innovation management tool. In addition to seeking corporate users for the tool, we're also continuing to develop a portfolio of specific vertical market instances of the tool that address critical social and business needs.

The Agile Innovation Master Plan

Adopting Agile Innovation and applying this Blockchain Design Sprint Workbook are important first steps in developing critical capabilities for long term success. The next step is to prepare your organization's Agile Innovation Master Plan, a comprehensive systems thinking approach that addresses the five key themes that are essential to success at innovation: Strategy, Portfolio, Process, Culture and Infrastructure. Or in language of the questions we probably learned even before we entered grade school—the why, what, how, who, and where of innovation.

The Agile master planning process is often developed as a series of five sprints, focusing sequentially on each key theme in turn. Each sprint lasts 4 to 10 days, and results in a working plan that describes your innovation strategy, the ideal design for your innovation portfolio, the optimization of your innovation process, etc.

Innovation
Master Plan

The process to improve the process through Systemic Innovation Management & Continuous Enhancement

Integrating these sprints results in a "working plan" that becomes a key element of your comprehensive innovation approach in which you'll apply essential innovation methodologies including ethnography, PAINstorming, multi-visioning, ideation reframing, the refined business model canvas, innovation storytelling, and the innospective process, all of which are powerful tools for creative thinking and innovative action.

Seminars and Workshops

The rapid development of the blockchain market space requires engagement in a constant learning process. To facilitate a high rate and high quality of information exchange, FutureLab offers seminars and workshops on the blockchain in which we address a very broad range of pertinent themes and topics. These sessions are great for familiarizing executives grasp the full potential impact of blockchains, and can also be used to design action plans, research agendas, and application portfolios.

Check us out at www.futurelabconsulting.com!

INDEX

About the Author

Moses Ma is the managing partner of FutureLab Consulting, an innovation consultancy that works with senior executives at global companies and organizations. He also runs a boutique venture incubator associated with FutureLab. As a technology visionary, he has been praised in Time Magazine and the New York Times. Over the years—he was a legendary games designer who created two of the world's best-selling computer games, including the world's first commercially successful Internet game; he took an uncapitalized software start-up and built it into one of the fastest growing and most profitable in the country; and he helped invent the concept of e-markets in business-to-business e-commerce. Moses was trained as a scientist and received a bachelor of science degree from Caltech in physics.

Made in the USA
Middletown, DE
08 March 2018